Say It With Symbols

Making Sense of Symbols

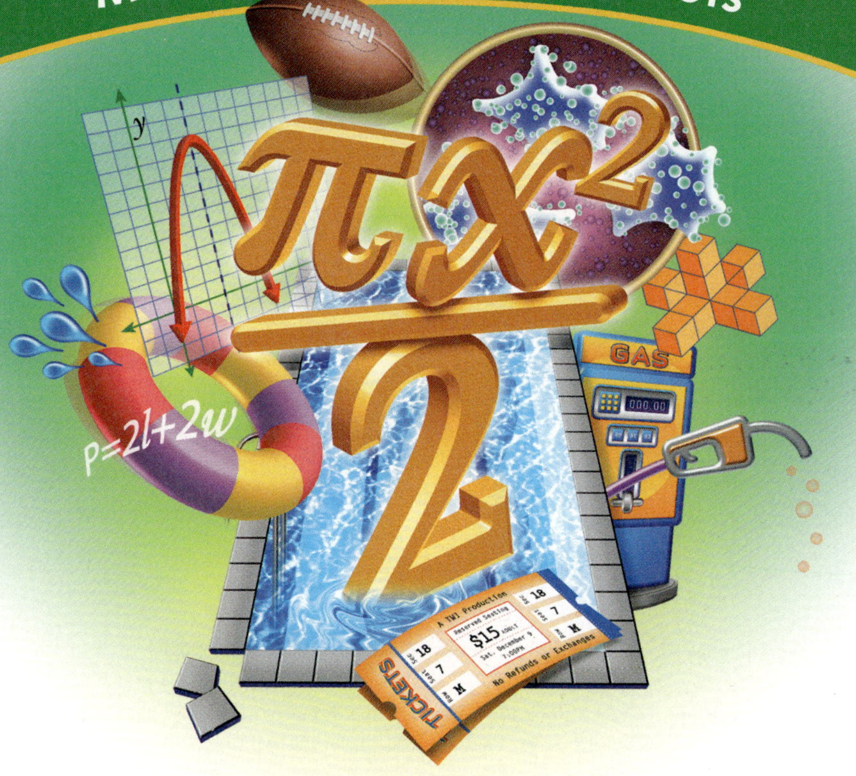

Glenda Lappan
James T. Fey
William M. Fitzgerald
Susan N. Friel
Elizabeth Difanis Phillips

Boston, Massachusetts · Glenview, Illinois · Shoreview, Minnesota · Upper Saddle River, New Jersey

Connected Mathematics™ was developed at Michigan State University with financial support from the Michigan State University Office of the Provost, Computing and Technology, and the College of Natural Science.

This material is based upon work supported by the National Science Foundation under Grant No. MDR 9150217 and Grant No. ESI 9986372. Opinions expressed are those of the authors and not necessarily those of the Foundation.

The Michigan State University authors and administration have agreed that all MSU royalties arising from this publication will be devoted to purposes supported by the MSU Mathematics Education Enrichment Fund.

Acknowledgments appear on page 97, which constitutes an extension of this copyright page.

13-digit ISBN 978-0-13-366155-2
10-digit ISBN 0-13-366155-5
2 3 4 5 6 7 8 9 10 11 10 09 08

Authors of Connected Mathematics

(from left to right) Glenda Lappan, Betty Phillips, Susan Friel, Bill Fitzgerald, Jim Fey

Glenda Lappan is a University Distinguished Professor in the Department of Mathematics at Michigan State University. Her research and development interests are in the connected areas of students' learning of mathematics and mathematics teachers' professional growth and change related to the development and enactment of K–12 curriculum materials.

James T. Fey is a Professor of Curriculum and Instruction and Mathematics at the University of Maryland. His consistent professional interest has been development and research focused on curriculum materials that engage middle and high school students in problem-based collaborative investigations of mathematical ideas and their applications.

William M. Fitzgerald (*Deceased*) was a Professor in the Department of Mathematics at Michigan State University. His early research was on the use of concrete materials in supporting student learning and led to the development of teaching materials for laboratory environments. Later he helped develop a teaching model to support student experimentation with mathematics.

Susan N. Friel is a Professor of Mathematics Education in the School of Education at the University of North Carolina at Chapel Hill. Her research interests focus on statistics education for middle-grade students and, more broadly, on teachers' professional development and growth in teaching mathematics K–8.

Elizabeth Difanis Phillips is a Senior Academic Specialist in the Mathematics Department of Michigan State University. She is interested in teaching and learning mathematics for both teachers and students. These interests have led to curriculum and professional development projects at the middle school and high school levels, as well as projects related to the teaching and learning of algebra across the grades.

CMP2 Development Staff

Teacher Collaborator in Residence

Yvonne Grant
Michigan State University

Administrative Assistant

Judith Martus Miller
Michigan State University

Production and Field Site Manager

Lisa Keller
Michigan State University

Technical and Editorial Support

Brin Keller, Peter Lappan, Jim Laser, Michael Masterson, Stacey Miceli

Assessment Team

June Bailey and **Debra Sobko** (Apollo Middle School, Rochester, New York), **George Bright** (University of North Carolina, Greensboro), **Gwen Ranzau Campbell** (Sunrise Park Middle School, White Bear Lake, Minnesota), **Holly DeRosia, Kathy Dole,** and **Teri Keusch** (Portland Middle School, Portland, Michigan), **Mary Beth Schmitt** (Traverse City East Junior High School, Traverse City, Michigan), **Genni Steele** (Central Middle School, White Bear Lake, Minnesota), **Jacqueline Stewart** (Okemos, Michigan), **Elizabeth Tye** (Magnolia Junior High School, Magnolia, Arkansas)

Development Assistants

At Lansing Community College *Undergraduate Assistant:* **James Brinegar**

At Michigan State University *Graduate Assistants:* **Dawn Berk, Emily Bouck, Bulent Buyukbozkirli, Kuo-Liang Chang, Christopher Danielson, Srinivasa Dharmavaram, Deb Johanning, Kelly Rivette, Sarah Sword, Tat Ming Sze, Marie Turini, Jeffrey Wanko;** *Undergraduate Assistants:* **Daniel Briggs, Jeffrey Chapin, Jade Corsé, Elisha Hardy, Alisha Harold, Elizabeth Keusch, Julia Letoutchaia, Karen Loeffler, Brian Oliver, Carl Oliver, Evonne Pedawi, Lauren Rebrovich**

At the University of Maryland *Graduate Assistants:* **Kim Harris Bethea, Kara Karch**

At the University of North Carolina (Chapel Hill) *Graduate Assistants:* **Mark Ellis, Trista Stearns;** *Undergraduate Assistant:* **Daniel Smith**

Advisory Board for CMP2

Thomas Banchoff
Professor of Mathematics
Brown University
Providence, Rhode Island

Anne Bartel
Mathematics Coordinator
Minneapolis Public Schools
Minneapolis, Minnesota

Hyman Bass
Professor of Mathematics
University of Michigan
Ann Arbor, Michigan

Joan Ferrini-Mundy
Associate Dean of the College of Natural Science; Professor
Michigan State University
East Lansing, Michigan

James Hiebert
Professor
University of Delaware
Newark, Delaware

Susan Hudson Hull
Charles A. Dana Center
University of Texas
Austin, Texas

Michele Luke
Mathematics Curriculum Coordinator
West Junior High
Minnetonka, Minnesota

Kay McClain
Professor of Mathematics Education
Vanderbilt University
Nashville, Tennessee

Edward Silver
Professor; Chair of Educational Studies
University of Michigan
Ann Arbor, Michigan

Judith Sowder
Professor Emerita
San Diego State University
San Diego, California

Lisa Usher
Mathematics Resource Teacher
California Academy of Mathematics and Science
San Pedro, California

Field Test Sites for CMP2

During the development of the revised edition of *Connected Mathematics* (CMP2), more than 100 classroom teachers have field-tested materials at 49 school sites in 12 states and the District of Columbia. This classroom testing occurred over three academic years (2001 through 2004), allowing careful study of the effectiveness of each of the 24 units that comprise the program. A special thanks to the students and teachers at these pilot schools.

Arkansas

Magnolia Public Schools
Kittena Bell*, Judith Trowell*; *Central Elementary School:* Maxine Broom, Betty Eddy, Tiffany Fallin, Bonnie Flurry, Carolyn Monk, Elizabeth Tye; *Magnolia Junior High School:* Monique Bryan, Ginger Cook, David Graham, Shelby Lamkin

Colorado

Boulder Public Schools
Nevin Platt Middle School: Judith Koenig

St. Vrain Valley School District, Longmont
Westview Middle School: Colleen Beyer, Kitty Canupp, Ellie Decker*, Tanya deNobrega, Peggy McCarthy, Cindy Payne, Ericka Pilon, Andrew Roberts

District of Columbia

Capitol Hill Day School: Ann Lawrence

Georgia

University of Georgia, Athens
Brad Findell

Madison Public Schools
Morgan County Middle School: Renee Burgdorf, Lynn Harris, Nancy Kurtz, Carolyn Stewart

Maine

Falmouth Public Schools
Falmouth Middle School: Donna Erikson, Joyce Hebert, Paula Hodgkins, Rick Hogan, David Legere, Cynthia Martin, Barbara Stiles, Shawn Towle*

Michigan

Portland Public Schools
Portland Middle School: Mark Braun, Holly DeRosia, Kathy Dole*, Angie Foote, Teri Keusch, Tammi Wardwell

Traverse City Area Public Schools
Bertha Vos Elementary: Kristin Sak; *Central Grade School:* Michelle Clark; Jody Meyers; *Eastern Elementary:* Karrie Tufts; *Interlochen Elementary:* Mary McGee-Cullen; *Long Lake Elementary:* Julie Faulkner*, Charlie Maxbauer, Katherine Sleder; *Norris Elementary:* Hope Slanaker; *Oak Park Elementary:* Jessica Steed; *Traverse Heights Elementary:* Jennifer Wolfert; *Westwoods Elementary:* Nancy Conn; *Old Mission Peninsula School:* Deb Larimer; *Traverse City East Junior High:* Ivanka Berkshire, Ruthanne Kladder, Jan Palkowski, Jane Peterson, Mary Beth Schmitt; *Traverse City West Junior High:* Dan Fouch*, Ray Fouch

Sturgis Public Schools
Sturgis Middle School: Ellen Eisele

Minnesota

Burnsville School District 191
Hidden Valley Elementary: Stephanie Cin, Jane McDevitt

Hopkins School District 270
Alice Smith Elementary: Sandra Cowing, Kathleen Gustafson, Martha Mason, Scott Stillman; *Eisenhower Elementary:* Chad Bellig, Patrick Berger, Nancy Glades, Kye Johnson, Shane Wasserman, Victoria Wilson; *Gatewood Elementary:* Sarah Ham, Julie Kloos, Janine Pung, Larry Wade; *Glen Lake Elementary:* Jacqueline Cramer, Kathy Hering, Cecelia Morris, Robb Trenda; *Katherine Curren Elementary:* Diane Bancroft, Sue DeWit, John Wilson; *L. H. Tanglen Elementary:* Kevin Athmann, Lisa Becker, Mary LaBelle, Kathy Rezac, Roberta Severson; *Meadowbrook Elementary:* Jan Gauger, Hildy Shank, Jessica Zimmerman; *North Junior High:* Laurel Hahn, Kristin Lee, Jodi Markuson, Bruce Mestemacher, Laurel Miller, Bonnie Rinker, Jeannine Salzer, Sarah Shafer, Cam Stottler; *West Junior High:* Alicia Beebe, Kristie Earl, Nobu Fujii, Pam Georgetti, Susan Gilbert, Regina Nelson Johnson, Debra Lindstrom, Michele Luke*, Jon Sorenson

Minneapolis School District 1
Ann Sullivan K-8 School: Bronwyn Collins; Anne Bartel* (Curriculum and Instruction Office)

Wayzata School District 284
Central Middle School: Sarajane Myers, Dan Nielsen, Tanya Ravnholdt

White Bear Lake School District 624
Central Middle School: Amy Jorgenson, Michelle Reich, Brenda Sammon

New York

New York City Public Schools
IS 89: Yelena Aynbinder, Chi-Man Ng, Nina Rapaport, Joel Spengler, Phyllis Tam*, Brent Wyso; *Wagner Middle School:* Jason Appel, Intissar Fernandez, Yee Gee Get, Richard Goldstein, Irving Marcus, Sue Norton, Bernadita Owens, Jennifer Rehn*, Kevin Yuhas

---

* indicates a Field Test Site Coordinator

Ohio

Talawanda School District, Oxford
Talawanda Middle School: Teresa Abrams, Larry Brock, Heather Brosey, Julie Churchman, Monna Even, Karen Fitch, Bob George, Amanda Klee, Pat Meade, Sandy Montgomery, Barbara Sherman, Lauren Steidl

Miami University
Jeffrey Wanko*

Springfield Public Schools
Rockway School: Jim Mamer

Pennsylvania

Pittsburgh Public Schools
Kenneth Labuskes, Marianne O'Connor, Mary Lynn Raith*; *Arthur J. Rooney Middle School:* David Hairston, Stamatina Mousetis, Alfredo Zangaro; *Frick International Studies Academy:* Suzanne Berry, Janet Falkowski, Constance Finseth, Romika Hodge, Frank Machi; *Reizenstein Middle School:* Jeff Baldwin, James Brautigam, Lorena Burnett, Glen Cobbett, Michael Jordan, Margaret Lazur, Melissa Munnell, Holly Neely, Ingrid Reed, Dennis Reft

Texas

Austin Independent School District
Bedichek Middle School: Lisa Brown, Jennifer Glasscock, Vicki Massey

El Paso Independent School District
Cordova Middle School: Armando Aguirre, Anneliesa Durkes, Sylvia Guzman, Pat Holguin*, William Holguin, Nancy Nava, Laura Orozco, Michelle Peña, Roberta Rosen, Patsy Smith, Jeremy Wolf

Plano Independent School District
Patt Henry, James Wohlgehagen*; *Frankford Middle School:* Mandy Baker, Cheryl Butsch, Amy Dudley, Betsy Eshelman, Janet Greene, Cort Haynes, Kathy Letchworth, Kay Marshall, Kelly McCants, Amy Reck, Judy Scott, Syndy Snyder, Lisa Wang; *Wilson Middle School:* Darcie Bane, Amanda Bedenko, Whitney Evans, Tonelli Hatley, Sarah (Becky) Higgs, Kelly Johnston, Rebecca McElligott, Kay Neuse, Cheri Slocum, Kelli Straight

Washington

Evergreen School District
Shahala Middle School: Nicole Abrahamsen, Terry Coon*, Carey Doyle, Sheryl Drechsler, George Gemma, Gina Helland, Amy Hilario, Darla Lidyard, Sean McCarthy, Tilly Meyer, Willow Neuwelt, Todd Parsons, Brian Pederson, Stan Posey, Shawn Scott, Craig Sjoberg, Lynette Sundstrom, Charles Switzer, Luke Youngblood

Wisconsin

Beaver Dam Unified School District
Beaver Dam Middle School: Jim Braemer, Jeanne Frick, Jessica Greatens, Barbara Link, Dennis McCormick, Karen Michels, Nancy Nichols*, Nancy Palm, Shelly Stelsel, Susan Wiggins

---

* indicates a Field Test Site Coordinator

Reviews of CMP to Guide Development of CMP2

Before writing for CMP2 began or field tests were conducted, the first edition of *Connected Mathematics* was submitted to the mathematics faculties of school districts from many parts of the country and to 80 individual reviewers for extensive comments.

School District Survey Reviews of CMP

Arizona
Madison School District #38 (Phoenix)

Arkansas
Cabot School District, Little Rock School District, Magnolia School District

California
Los Angeles Unified School District

Colorado
St. Vrain Valley School District (Longmont)

Florida
Leon County Schools (Tallahassee)

Illinois
School District #21 (Wheeling)

Indiana
Joseph L. Block Junior High (East Chicago)

Kentucky
Fayette County Public Schools (Lexington)

Maine
Selection of Schools

Massachusetts
Selection of Schools

Michigan
Sparta Area Schools

Minnesota
Hopkins School District

Texas
Austin Independent School District, The El Paso Collaborative for Academic Excellence, Plano Independent School District

Wisconsin
Platteville Middle School

Individual Reviewers of CMP

Arkansas
Deborah Cramer; Robby Frizzell *(Taylor)*; Lowell Lynde *(University of Arkansas, Monticello)*; Leigh Manzer *(Norfork)*; Lynne Roberts *(Emerson High School, Emerson)*; Tony Timms *(Cabot Public Schools)*; Judith Trowell *(Arkansas Department of Higher Education)*

California
José Alcantar *(Gilroy)*; Eugenie Belcher *(Gilroy)*; Marian Pasternack *(Lowman M. S. T. Center, North Hollywood)*; Susana Pezoa *(San Jose)*; Todd Rabusin *(Hollister)*; Margaret Siegfried *(Ocala Middle School, San Jose)*; Polly Underwood *(Ocala Middle School, San Jose)*

Colorado
Janeane Golliher *(St. Vrain Valley School District, Longmont)*; Judith Koenig *(Nevin Platt Middle School, Boulder)*

Florida
Paige Loggins *(Swift Creek Middle School, Tallahassee)*

Illinois
Jan Robinson *(School District #21, Wheeling)*

Indiana
Frances Jackson *(Joseph L. Block Junior High, East Chicago)*

Kentucky
Natalee Feese *(Fayette County Public Schools, Lexington)*

Maine
Betsy Berry *(Maine Math & Science Alliance, Augusta)*

Maryland
Joseph Gagnon *(University of Maryland, College Park)*; Paula Maccini *(University of Maryland, College Park)*

Massachusetts
George Cobb *(Mt. Holyoke College, South Hadley)*; Cliff Kanold *(University of Massachusetts, Amherst)*

Michigan
Mary Bouck *(Farwell Area Schools)*; Carol Dorer *(Slauson Middle School, Ann Arbor)*; Carrie Heaney *(Forsythe Middle School, Ann Arbor)*; Ellen Hopkins *(Clague Middle School, Ann Arbor)*; Teri Keusch *(Portland Middle School, Portland)*; Valerie Mills *(Oakland Schools, Waterford)*; Mary Beth Schmitt *(Traverse City East Junior High, Traverse City)*; Jack Smith *(Michigan State University, East Lansing)*; Rebecca Spencer *(Sparta Middle School, Sparta)*; Ann Marie Nicoll Turner *(Tappan Middle School, Ann Arbor)*; Scott Turner *(Scarlett Middle School, Ann Arbor)*

Minnesota
Margarita Alvarez *(Olson Middle School, Minneapolis)*; Jane Amundson *(Nicollet Junior High, Burnsville)*; Anne Bartel *(Minneapolis Public Schools)*; Gwen Ranzau Campbell *(Sunrise Park Middle School, White Bear Lake)*; Stephanie Cin *(Hidden Valley Elementary, Burnsville)*; Joan Garfield *(University of Minnesota, Minneapolis)*; Gretchen Hall *(Richfield Middle School, Richfield)*; Jennifer Larson *(Olson Middle School, Minneapolis)*; Michele Luke *(West Junior High, Minnetonka)*; Jeni Meyer *(Richfield Junior High, Richfield)*; Judy Pfingsten *(Inver Grove Heights Middle School, Inver Grove Heights)*; Sarah Shafer *(North Junior High, Minnetonka)*; Genni Steele *(Central Middle School, White Bear Lake)*; Victoria Wilson *(Eisenhower Elementary, Hopkins)*; Paul Zorn *(St. Olaf College, Northfield)*

New York
Debra Altenau-Bartolino *(Greenwich Village Middle School, New York)*; Doug Clements *(University of Buffalo)*; Francis Curcio *(New York University, New York)*; Christine Dorosh *(Clinton School for Writers, Brooklyn)*; Jennifer Rehn *(East Side Middle School, New York)*; Phyllis Tam *(IS 89 Lab School, New York)*; Marie Turini *(Louis Armstrong Middle School, New York)*; Lucy West *(Community School District 2, New York)*; Monica Witt *(Simon Baruch Intermediate School 104, New York)*

Pennsylvania
Robert Aglietti *(Pittsburgh)*; Sharon Mihalich *(Pittsburgh)*; Jennifer Plumb *(South Hills Middle School, Pittsburgh)*; Mary Lynn Raith *(Pittsburgh Public Schools)*

Texas
Michelle Bittick *(Austin Independent School District)*; Margaret Cregg *(Plano Independent School District)*; Sheila Cunningham *(Klein Independent School District)*; Judy Hill *(Austin Independent School District)*; Patricia Holguin *(El Paso Independent School District)*; Bonnie McNemar *(Arlington)*; Kay Neuse *(Plano Independent School District)*; Joyce Polanco *(Austin Independent School District)*; Marge Ramirez *(University of Texas at El Paso)*; Pat Rossman *(Baker Campus, Austin)*; Cindy Schimek *(Houston)*; Cynthia Schneider *(Charles A. Dana Center, University of Texas at Austin)*; Uri Treisman *(Charles A. Dana Center, University of Texas at Austin)*; Jacqueline Weilmuenster *(Grapevine–Colleyville Independent School District)*; LuAnn Weynand *(San Antonio)*; Carmen Whitman *(Austin Independent School District)*; James Wohlgehagen *(Plano Independent School District)*

Washington
Ramesh Gangolli *(University of Washington, Seattle)*

Wisconsin
Susan Lamon *(Marquette University, Hales Corner)*; Steve Reinhart *(retired, Chippewa Falls Middle School, Eau Claire)*

Table of Contents

Say It With Symbols
Making Sense of Symbols

Say It With Symbols

Making Sense of Symbols

In-ground swimming pools are often surrounded by borders of tiles. How many border tiles N do you need to surround the square pool in the figure at the left?

The school choir is selling boxes of greeting cards to raise money for a trip.

How many boxes must the choir sell to make a $200 profit?

Perform the following operations on the first eight odd numbers.

- Pick an odd whole number.
- Square it.
- Subtract 1.

What patterns do you see in the resulting numbers?

You have used many powerful tools, including graphs, tables, and equations, to represent relationships among variables. Graphs allow you to see the shape of a relationship. They also help you identify intercepts and maximum and minimum points. Tables help you observe patterns of change in the values of the variables. Equations give you an efficient way to generalize relationships.

In *Say It With Symbols*, you will concentrate on symbolic expressions and equations. You will see that different ways of reasoning about a situation can lead to different but equivalent expressions. You will use mathematical properties to rewrite expressions, and you may discover that an equivalent expression allows you to think about a problem in a new way. And, you will learn new ways to solve equations. Pools are used as a context throughout this unit to introduce these ideas.

As you work through the unit, you will solve problems similar to those on the previous page.

Mathematical Highlights

Making Sense of Symbols

Algebra provides ideas and symbols for expressing information about quantitative variables and relationships. In *Say It With Symbols*, you will solve problems designed to develop your understanding and skill in using symbolic expressions and equations in algebra.

You will learn how to

- Represent patterns and relationships in symbolic forms
- Determine when different symbolic expressions are mathematically equivalent
- Write algebraic expressions in useful equivalent forms
- Combine symbolic expressions using algebraic operations
- Analyze expressions or equations to determine the patterns of change in the tables and graphs that the equation represents
- Solve linear and quadratic equations using symbolic reasoning
- Use algebraic reasoning to validate generalizations and conjectures

As you work on problems in this unit, ask yourself questions about situations that involve symbolic expressions and equations.

What expression or equation represents the pattern or relationship in a context?

Can you write an equivalent expression for a given expression to provide new information about a relationship?

What operations can transform a given equation or expression into an equivalent form that can be used to answer a question?

How can symbolic reasoning help confirm a conjecture?

Investigation 1

Equivalent Expressions

When you want to communicate an idea in words, you can usually express it in many ways. All the statements below communicate the same information about Mika and Jim.

- Jim is older than Mika.
- Mika is younger than Jim.
- Jim was born before Mika.
- Mika was born after Jim.

Can you think of other ways to express the same idea?

Symbolic expressions, formulas, and equations are valuable tools in mathematics. The formula $P = 2L + 2W$ gives directions for calculating the perimeter of any rectangle with length L and width W.

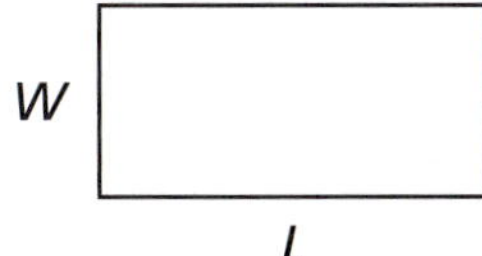

Since you can usually think about a situation in more than one way, you can often express the situation in symbols in more than one way.

Getting Ready for Problem  1.1

Jim says the perimeter of the rectangle above is $P = 2(L + W)$. Mika says the perimeter is $P = 2L + 2W$.

- Why do you think Jim used parentheses in his equation?
- Are the expressions $2L + 2W$ and $2(L + W)$ *equivalent*? Do they produce the same perimeter for any given pair of lengths and widths? Explain your reasoning.

Since $2(L + W)$ and $2L + 2W$ represent the same quantity (the perimeter of a rectangle), they are **equivalent expressions.** This investigation explores situations in which a quantity is described with several different, but equivalent, expressions. The question is:

How can we determine if two expressions are equivalent?

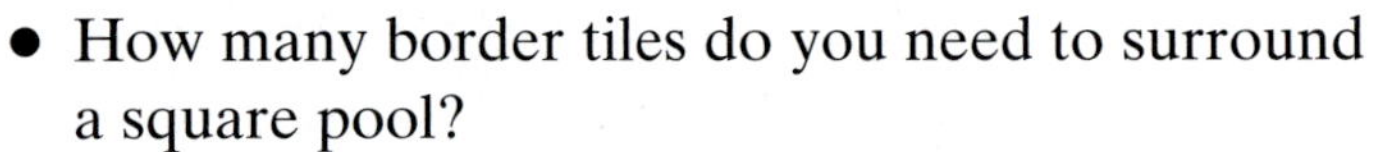

1.1 Tiling Pools

In-ground pools are often surrounded by borders of tiles. The Custom Pool Company gets orders for square pools of different sizes. For example, the pool at the right has side lengths of 5 feet and is surrounded by square border tiles. All Custom Pool border tiles measure 1 foot on each side.

- How many border tiles do you need to surround a square pool?

Problem 1.1 Writing Equivalent Expressions

In order to calculate the number of tiles needed for a project, the Custom Pool manager wants an equation relating the number of border tiles to the size of the pool.

A. **1.** Write an expression for the number of border tiles N based on the side length s of a square pool.

2. Write a different but equivalent expression for the number of tiles N needed to surround such a square pool.

3. Explain why your two expressions for the number of border tiles are equivalent.

B. **1.** Use each expression in Question A to write an equation for the number of border tiles N. Make a table and a graph for each equation.

2. Based on your table and graph, are the two expressions for the number of border tiles in Question A equivalent? Explain.

C. Is the relationship between the side length of the pool and the number of border tiles linear, exponential, quadratic, or none of these? Explain.

ACE Homework starts on page 12.

1.2 Thinking in Different Ways

When Takashi reported his ideas about an equation relating N and s in Problem 1.1, he made the following sketch.

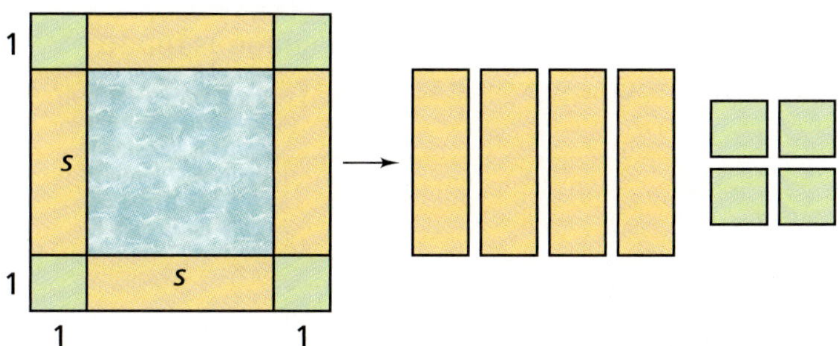

- What equation do you think Takashi wrote to relate N and s?

Problem 1.2 Determining Equivalence

A. Four students in Takashi's class came up with different equations for counting the number of border tiles. For each equation, make a sketch that shows how the student might have been thinking about the border of the pool.

1. Stella's equation: $N = 4(s + 1)$
2. Jeri's equation: $N = s + s + s + s + 4$
3. Hank's equation: $N = 4(s + 2)$
4. Sal's equation: $N = 2s + 2(s + 2)$

B. Use each equation in Question A to find the number of border tiles needed for a square pool with a side length of 10 feet. Can you conclude from your results that all the expressions for the number of tiles are equivalent? Explain your reasoning.

C. Which of the expressions for the number of border tiles in Question A are equivalent to Takashi's expression? Explain.

ACE **Homework starts on page 12.**

active math online
For: Algebra Tools Activity
Visit: PHSchool.com
Web Code: apd-6102

1.3 The Community Pool Problem

In this problem, we will interpret symbolic statements and use them to make predictions.

A community center is building a pool, part indoor and part outdoor. A diagram of the indoor part of the pool is shown. The indoor shape is made from a half-circle with radius x and a rectangle with length $4x$.

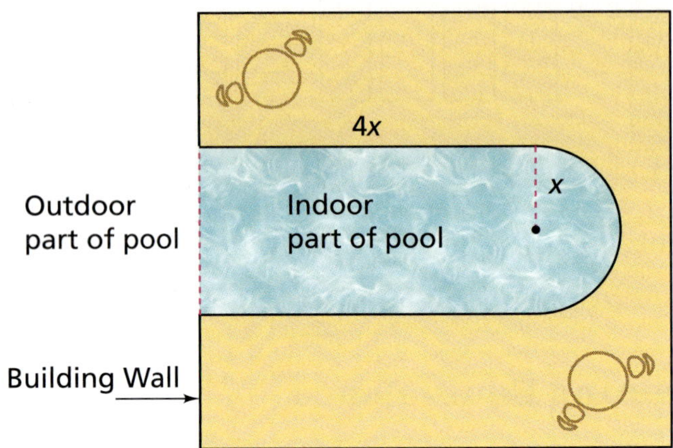

Problem 1.3 Interpreting Expressions

The exact dimensions of the community center pool are not available, but the area A of the whole pool is given by the equation:

$$A = x^2 + \frac{\pi x^2}{2} + 8x^2 + \frac{\pi x^2}{4}$$

A. Which part of the expression for area represents

  1. the area of the indoor part of the pool? Explain.

  2. the area of the outdoor part of the pool? Explain.

B. **1.** Make a sketch of the outdoor part. Label the dimensions.

  2. If possible, draw another shape for the outdoor part of the pool. If not, explain why not.

C. Stella and Jeri each rewrote the expression for the area of the outdoor part of the pool to help them make a sketch.

$$\text{Stella: } x^2 + \frac{\pi x^2}{8} + \frac{\pi x^2}{8}$$

$$\text{Jeri: } \left(\frac{1}{2}x\right)\left(2x\right) + \frac{\pi x^2}{4}$$

1. Explain the reasoning each person may have used to write their expression.
2. Decide if these expressions are equivalent to the original expression in Question A, part (2). Explain your reasoning.

D. Does the equation for the area of the pool represent a linear, exponential, or quadratic relationship, or none of these? Explain.

ACE **Homework starts on page 12.**

1.4 Diving In

In the pool tile problems, you found patterns that could be represented by several different but equivalent symbolic expressions, such as:

$$4s + 4$$
$$4(s + 1)$$
$$s + s + s + s + 4$$
$$2s + 2(s + 2)$$

The equivalence of these expressions can be shown with arrangements of tiles. Equivalence also follows from properties of numbers and operations.

An important property is the **Distributive Property:**

For any real numbers a, b, and c:

$$a(b + c) = ab + ac \text{ and } a(b - c) = ab - ac$$

For example, this property guarantees that $4(s + 1) = 4s + 4$ for any s.

We say that $a(b + c)$ and $4(s + 1)$ are in *factored form* and $ab + ac$ and $4s + 4$ are in *expanded form.*

The next problem reviews the Distributive Property.

Getting Ready for Problem 1.4

Swimming pools are sometimes divided into sections that are used for different purposes. A pool may have a section for swimming laps and a section for diving, or a section for experienced swimmers and a section for small children.

Below are diagrams of pools with swimming and diving sections. The dimensions are in meters.

1. 30; x, 10

2. x; 25, x

3. x, 2; x, 3

4.

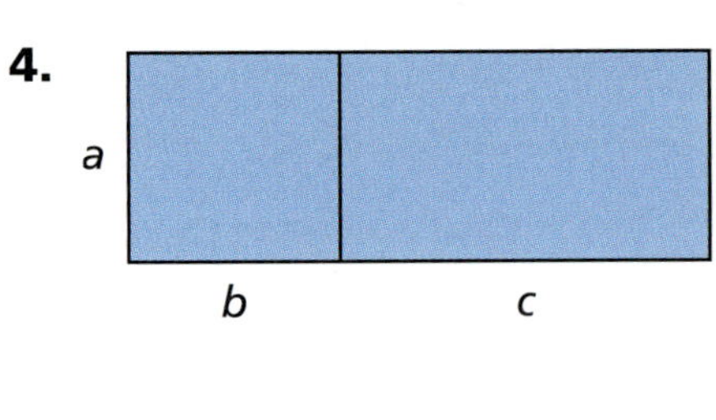

- For each pool, write two different but equivalent expressions for the total area.
- Explain how these diagrams and expressions illustrate the Distributive Property.

The Distributive Property, as well as the Commutative Property and other properties for numbers, are useful for writing equivalent expressions. The Commutative Property states that $a + b = b + a$ and $ab = ba$, where a and b are real numbers. These properties were discussed in previous units.

Problem 1.4 Revisiting the Distributive Property

A. Write each expression in expanded form.

1. $3(x + 5)$

2. $2(3x - 10)$

3. $2x(x + 5)$

4. $(x + 2)(x + 5)$

B. Write each expression in factored form.

1. $12 + 24x$

2. $x + x + x + 6$

3. $x^2 + 3x$

4. $x^2 + 4x + 3$

C. The following expressions all represent the number of border tiles N for a square pool with side length s.

$$4(s + 1)$$

$$s + s + s + s + 4$$

$$2s + 2(s + 2)$$

$$4(s + 2) - 4$$

$$(s + 2)^2 - s^2$$

Use the Distributive and Commutative properties to show that these expressions are equivalent.

D. Three of the following expressions are equivalent. Explain which expression is not equivalent to the other three.

1. $2x - 12x + 10$

2. $12x - 2x + 10$

3. $10 - 10x$

4. $10(1 - x)$

E. Copy each equation. Insert one set of parentheses in the expression to the left of the equal sign so that it is equivalent to the expression to the right of the equal sign.

1. $6p + 2 - 2p = 4p + 12$

2. $6p + 2 - 2p = 6p$

ACE **Homework starts on page 12.**

Applications Connections Extensions

Applications

1. **a.** How many 1-foot-square border tiles do you need to surround a pool that is 10 feet long and 5 feet wide?

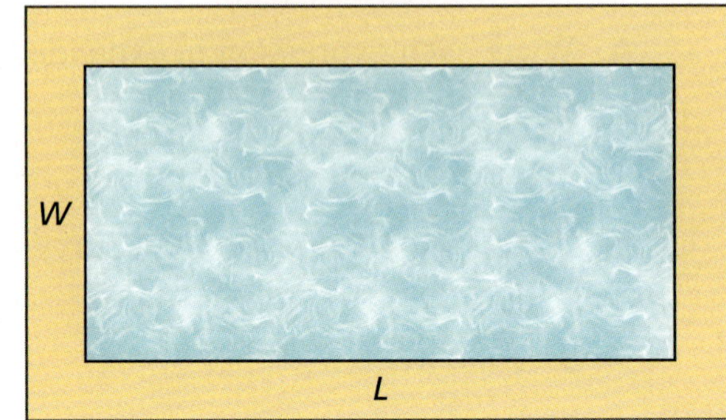

b. Write an equation for the number of border tiles needed to surround a pool L feet long and W feet wide.

c. Write a different but equivalent equation for the number of tiles needed in part (b). Explain why your equations are equivalent.

2. A square hot tub has sides of length s feet. A tiler creates a border by placing 1-foot-square tiles along the edges of the tub and triangular tiles at the corners, as shown. The tiler makes the triangular tiles by cutting the square tiles in half along a diagonal.

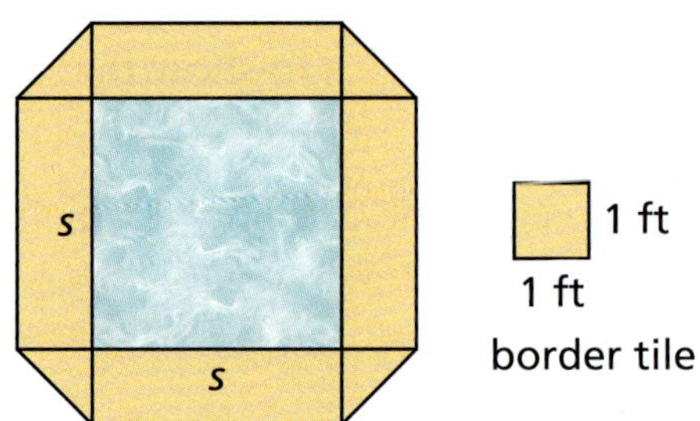

a. Suppose the hot tub has sides of length 7 feet. How many square tiles does the tiler need for the border?

b. Write an expression for the number of square tiles N needed to build this border for a square tub with sides of length s feet.

c. Write a different but equivalent expression for the number of tiles N. Explain why your expressions for the number of border tiles are equivalent.

d. Is the relationship between the number of tiles and side length linear, exponential, quadratic, or none of these? Explain.

3. A rectangular pool is L feet long and W feet wide. A tiler creates a border by placing 1-foot-square tiles along the edges of the pool and triangular tiles on the corners, as shown. The tiler makes the triangular tiles by cutting the square tiles in half along a diagonal.

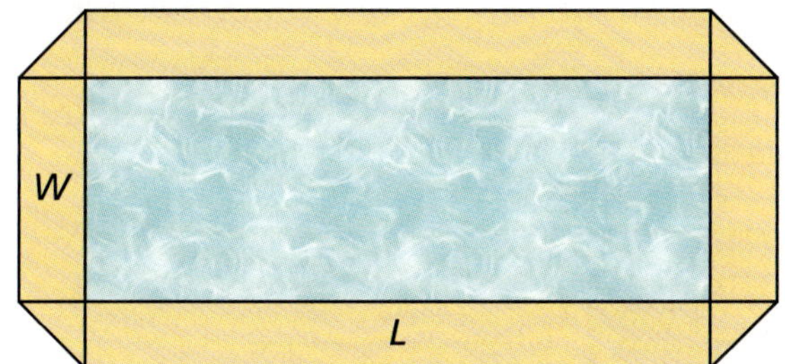

For: Help with Exercise 3
Web Code: ape-6103

Applications

a. Suppose the pool is 30 feet long and 20 feet wide. How many square tiles does the tiler need for the border?

b. Write two equations for the number of square tiles N needed to make this border for a pool L feet long and W feet wide.

c. Explain why your two equations are equivalent.

4. Below are three more expressions students wrote for the number of border tiles needed to surround the square pool in Problem 1.2.

$4\left(\frac{s}{2} + \frac{s}{4}\right) + 4 \qquad 2\left(s + 0.5\right) + 2\left(s + 1.5\right) \qquad 4\left[\frac{s + (s + 2)}{2}\right]$

a. Use each expression to find the number of border tiles N if $s = 0$.

b. Do you think the expressions are equivalent? Explain.

c. Use each expression to find the number of border tiles if $s = 12$. Has your answer to part (b) changed? Explain.

d. What can you say about testing specific values as a method for determining whether two or more expressions are equivalent?

5. A square surrounds a circle with a radius r. Each expression represents the area of part of this figure. Describe the shape or region each area represents.

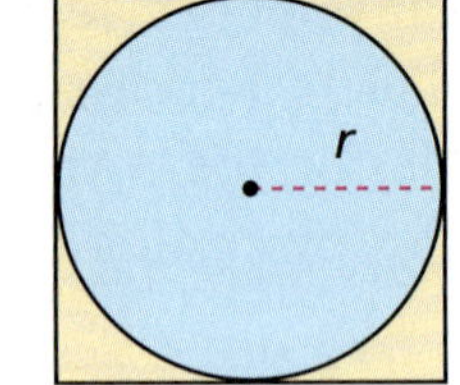

a. $4r^2 - \pi r^2$ **b.** $4r^2 - \frac{\pi r^2}{4}$

6. The dimensions of a pool are shown below.

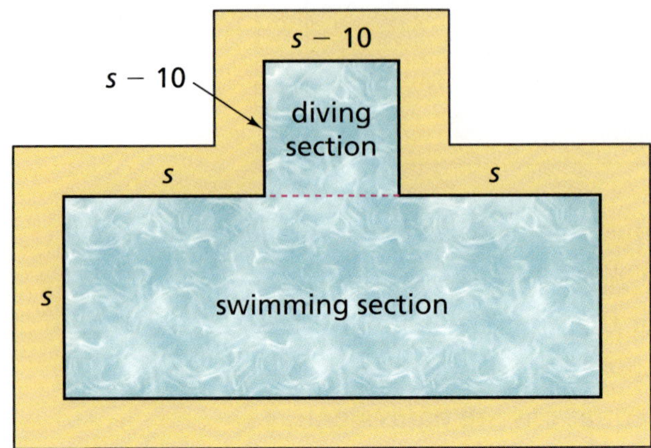

Each expression represents the surface area for part of the pool.

i. $s(3s - 10)$ **ii.** $(s - 10)^2$

iii. $2s^2 + s(s - 10)$ **iv.** $s^2 - 20s + 100$

a. Which expression(s) could represent the surface area of the diving section?

b. Which expression(s) could represent the surface area of the swimming section?

c. If you chose more than one expression for parts (a) and (b), show that they are equivalent.

d. Write an equation that represents the total surface area A of the pool.

e. What kind of relationship does the equation in part (d) represent?

Applications

For Exercises 7–9, complete parts (a)–(c).

a. For each expression, write an equation of the form $y = \textit{expression}$. Make a table and a graph of the two equations. Show x values from -5 to 5 on the graph.

b. Based on your table and graph, tell whether you think the two expressions are equivalent.

c. If you think the expressions are equivalent, use the properties you have learned in this investigation to verify their equivalence. If you think they are not equivalent, explain why.

7. $-3x + 6 + 5x$ and $6 + 2x$

8. $10 - 5x$ and $5x - 10$

9. $(3x + 4) + (2x - 3)$ and $5x + 1$

10. Use the Distributive Property to write each expression in expanded form.

a. $3(x + 7)$ **b.** $5(5 - x)$ **c.** $2(4x - 8)$ **d.** $(x + 4)(x + 2)$

11. Use the Distributive Property to write each expression in factored form.

a. $2x - 10x$ **b.** $2x + 6$ **c.** $14 - 7x$

12. Use the Distributive and Commutative properties to determine whether each pair of expressions is equivalent for all values of x.

a. $3x + 7x$ and $10x$ **b.** $5x$ and $5x - 10x$

c. $4(1 + 2x) - 3x$ and $5x + 4$ **d.** $5 - 3(2 - 4x)$ and $-1 + 12x$

13. Here is one way you might prove that $2(s + 2) + 2s$ is equivalent to $4s + 4$:

$$\begin{aligned}
&(1) \quad & 2(s + 2) + 2s &= 2s + 4 + 2s \\
&(2) \quad & &= 2s + 2s + 4 \\
&(3) \quad & &= (2 + 2)s + 4 \\
&(4) \quad & &= 4s + 4
\end{aligned}$$

What properties of numbers and operations justify each step?

14. Find three equivalent expressions for $6x + 3$.

For Exercises 15–17, copy the statement. Insert parentheses on the left side of the equation, if necessary, to make the statement true for all values of p.

15. $7 + 5p - p = 11p$

16. $7 + 5p - p = 7$

17. $7 + 5p - p = 7 + 4p$

Connections

In Exercises 18–23, each expression represents the area of a rectangle. Draw a divided rectangle for each expression. Label the lengths and areas. For Exercises 18–20, write an equivalent expression in expanded form. For Exercises 21–23, write an equivalent expression in factored form.

18. $x(x + 6)$ **19.** $x(x - 6)$ **20.** $x(5 + 1)$

21. $x^2 + 4x$ **22.** $x^2 - 2x$ **23.** $3x + 4x$

24. A circular pool with a radius of 4 feet has a 1-foot border.

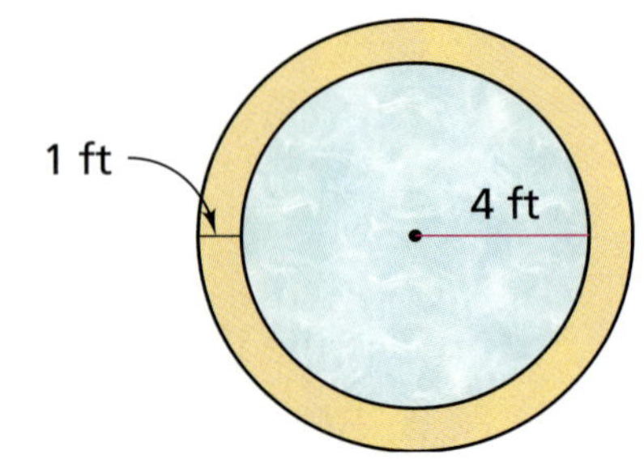

a. What is the surface area of the circular pool?

b. What is the surface area of the border?

c. Write an expression for the surface area of a circular pool with a radius of r feet.

d. Write an expression for the area of a 1-foot border around a circular pool with a radius of r feet.

25. Multiple Choice Which of the following expressions is equivalent to $m + m + m + m + m$?

A. $m + 5$ **B.** $5m$ **C.** m^5 **D.** $5(m + 1)$

26. Multiple Choice Which of the following expressions is equivalent to $a - b$, where a and b are any numbers?

F. $b - a$ **G.** $a + b$ **H.** $-a + b$ **J.** $-b + a$

For Exercises 27–32, draw and label a rectangle whose area is represented by the expression. For Exercises 27–29, write an equivalent expression in expanded form. For Exercises 30–32, write an equivalent expression in factored form.

27. $(x + 1)(x + 4)$ **28.** $(x + 5)(x + 6)$ **29.** $3x(5 + 2)$

30. $x^2 + x + 2x + 2$ **31.** $x^2 + 7x + 10$ **32.** $x^2 + 14x + 49$

Find each sum or difference.

33. $\frac{5}{7} - \frac{1}{3}$ **34.** $\frac{5}{2} + \frac{1}{3}$

35. $\frac{1}{2}x + \frac{1}{2}x$ **36.** $\frac{2}{3}x - \frac{1}{2}x$

Go Online
PHSchool.com
For: Multiple-Choice Skills Practice
Web Code: apa-6154

Find each sum, difference, product, or quotient.

37. 2×14

38. $-2 - (-14)$

39. $-2 \div (-14)$

40. $-6 \times (-11)$

41. $-6 + 11$

42. $6 - 11$

43. $-18(3x)$

44. $\frac{-24x}{-8}$

45. $-18x \div 3$

Find the greatest common factor for each pair of numbers.

46. 35 and 40

47. 36 and 12

48. 100 and 25

49. 42 and 9

50. Below is a diagram of Otter Middle School's outdoor track. The shape of the interior region (shaded green) is a rectangle with two half circles at each end.

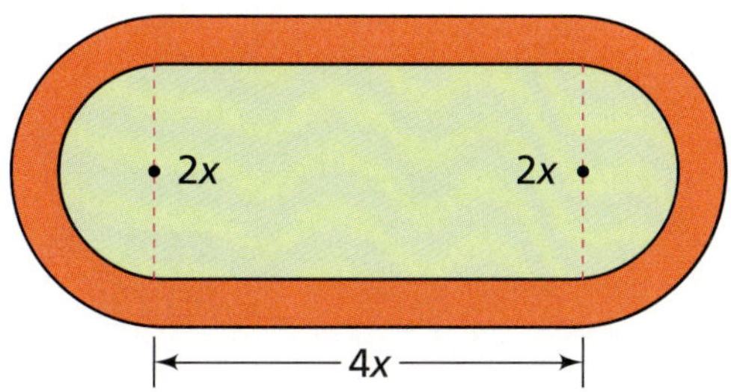

a. Find an expression that represents the area of the interior region.

b. Find the perimeter of the interior region as if you wanted to put a fence around it. Explain how you found your answer.

c. Write an expression equivalent to the one in part (b).

Connections

51. For Problem 1.2, Percy wrote the expression $8 + 4(s - 1)$ to represent the number of border tiles needed to surround a square pool with side length s.

a. Is this expression equivalent to the other expressions? Explain.

b. Four students used Percy's expression to calculate the number of border tiles needed for a pool with a side length of 6 feet. Which student performed the calculations correctly?

Stella

8 + 4(6 − 1) = 8 + 24 − 1
= 31 tiles

Hank

8 + 4(6 − 1) = 8 + 4(5)
= 8 + 20
= 28 tiles

Takashi

8 + 4(6 − 1) = 12 + (6 − 1)
= 12 + 5
= 17 tiles

Jackie

8 + 4(6 − 1) = 12(6 − 1)
= 12(5)
= 60 tiles

52. Lily invests D dollars in a money-market account that earns 10% interest per year. She does not plan on taking money out during the year. She writes the expression $D + 0.10D$ to represent the amount of money in the account at the end of one year.

a. Explain why this expression is correct.

b. Write an equivalent expression in factored form.

c. Suppose Lily invested $1,500. How much money will she have in her account at the end of one year?

For Exercises 53 and 54, use this information: The ski club is planning a trip for winter break. They write the equation $C = 200 + 10N$ to estimate the cost in dollars C of the trip for N students.

53. Duncan and Corey both use the equation to estimate the cost for 50 students. Duncan says the cost is \$10,500, and Corey says it is \$700.

a. Whose estimate is correct? Show your work.

b. How do you think Duncan and Corey found such different estimates if they both used the same equation?

54. a. Suppose 20 students go on the trip. What is the cost per student?

b. Write an equation for the cost per student S when N students go on the trip.

c. Use your equation to find the cost per student when 40 students go on the trip.

55. The pyramid and rectangular prism have the same base and height.

a. Find the volume of the pyramid.

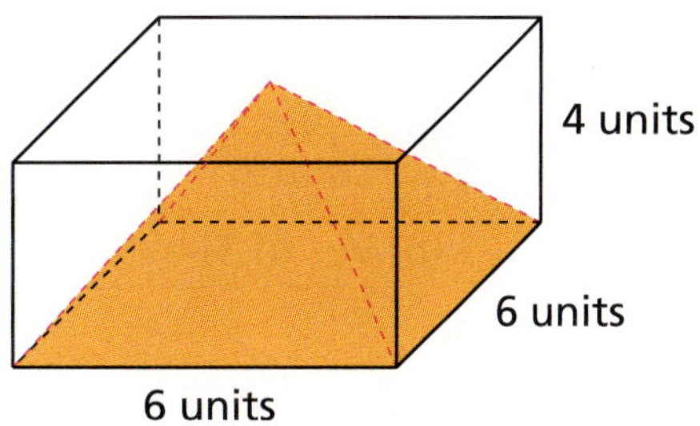

b. Draw a pyramid with a volume of $\left(\frac{1}{3}\right)\left(8\right)$ cubic units.

Hint: You might find it easier to draw the related prism first.

c. Draw a pyramid with a volume of $\left(\frac{1}{3}\right)\left(27\right)$ cubic units.

d. Find a possible height of a pyramid whose volume is $9x^3$ cubic units.

Connections

56. Below are two students' calculations for writing an equivalent expression for $10 - 4(x - 1) + 11 \times 3$.

a. Which student performed the calculations correctly?

b. What mistakes did the other student make?

Sarah

$$\begin{aligned} 10 - 4(x - 1) + 11 \times 3 &= 10 - 4x + 4 + 11 \times 3 \\ &= 10 - 4x + 4 + 33 \\ &= 10 - 4x + 37 \\ &= 10 + 37 - 4x \\ &= 47 - 4x \end{aligned}$$

Emily

$$\begin{aligned} 10 - 4(x - 1) + 11 \times 3 &= 10 - 4x + 4 + 11 \times 3 \\ &= 10 - 4x + 15 \times 3 \\ &= 25 - 4x \times 3 \\ &= 25 - 12x \end{aligned}$$

Extensions

57. Percy wants to write an equation for the number of tiles needed to surround a square pool with sides of length s feet. He makes a table for pools with sides of length 1, 2, 3, 4, and 5 feet. Then he uses the patterns in his table to write the equation $N = 8 + 4(s - 1)$.

Border Tiles

Side Length	1	2	3	4	5
Number of Tiles	8	12	16	20	24

a. What patterns does Percy see in his table?

b. Is Percy's expression for the number of tiles equivalent to $4(s + 1)$, Stella's expression in Problem 1.2? Explain.

58. Two expressions for the number of border tiles for the pool at the right are given.

$2(s + 0.5) + 2(s + 1.5)$

$4\left[\frac{s + (s + 2)}{2}\right]$

Sketch a picture that illustrates each expression.

59. The *Expression Puzzles* below all start with the original expression $2n - 3 + 4n + 6n + 1$. Each one ends with a different expression.

a. Solve each puzzle by inserting one set of parentheses in the original expression so that it is equivalent to the desired result.

b. Show that your expression is equivalent to the desired result. Justify each step.

Expression Puzzles

Puzzle	Original Expression	Desired Result
1	$2n - 3 + 4n + 6n + 1$	$12n - 5$
2	$2n - 3 + 4n + 6n + 1$	$12n + 3$
3	$2n - 3 + 4n + 6n + 1$	$12n - 2$
4	$2n - 3 + 4n + 6n + 1$	$n + 1$

Mathematical Reflections 1

In this investigation, you found different but equivalent expressions to represent a quantity in a relationship. These questions will help you summarize what you have learned.

Think about your answers to these questions. Discuss your ideas with other students and your teacher. Then write a summary of your findings in your notebook.

1. What does it mean to say that two expressions are equivalent?
2. Explain how the Distributive and Commutative properties can be used to write equivalent expressions.
3. Explain how the Distributive and Commutative properties can be used to show that two or more expressions are equivalent.

Investigation 2

Combining Expressions

In the last investigation, you found several ways to write equivalent expressions to describe a quantity. You also learned several ways to show that two expressions are equivalent. We will continue to answer the questions:

- Are the expressions equivalent? Why?
- What information does each equivalent expression represent?

We will also look at ways to create new expressions and to answer the question:

- What are the advantages and disadvantages of using one equation rather than two or more equations to represent a situation?

2.1 Walking Together

In *Moving Straight Ahead*, Leanne, Gilberto, and Alana enter a walkathon as a team. This means that each person will walk the same number of kilometers. The walkathon organizers offer a prize to the three-person team that raises the most money.

- Leanne has walkathon pledges from 16 sponsors. All of her sponsors pledge \$10 regardless of how far she walks.
- Gilberto has pledges from 7 sponsors. Each sponsor pledges \$2 for each kilometer he walks.
- Alana has pledges from 11 sponsors. Each sponsor pledges \$5 plus \$0.50 for each kilometer she walks.

Problem 2.1 Adding Expressions

A. 1. Write equations to represent the money M that each student will raise for walking x kilometers.

a. $M_{\text{Leanne}} = ■$

b. $M_{\text{Gilberto}} = ■$

c. $M_{\text{Alana}} = ■$

2. Write an equation for the total money M_{total} raised by the three-person team for walking x kilometers.

B. 1. Write an expression that is equivalent to the expression for the total amount in Question A, part (2). Explain why it is equivalent.

2. What information does this new expression represent about the situation?

3. Suppose each person walks 10 kilometers. Explain which expression(s) you would use to calculate the total amount of money raised.

C. Are the relationships between kilometers walked and money raised linear, exponential, quadratic, or none of these? Explain.

ACE Homework starts on page 28.

2.2 Predicting Profit

The manager of the Water City amusement park uses data collected over the past several years to write equations that will help her make predictions about the daily operations of the park.

The daily concession-stand profit in dollars P depends on the number of visitors V. The manager writes the equation below to model this relationship.

$$P = 2.50V - 500$$

She uses the equation below to predict the number of visitors V based on the probability of rain R.

$$V = 600 - 500R$$

- What information might each of the numbers in the equations represent?

Problem 2.2 Substituting Equivalent Expressions

A. **1.** Suppose the probability of rain is 25%. What profit can the concession stand expect? Explain.

2. What was the probability of rain if the profit expected is \$625? Explain your reasoning.

B. **1.** Write an equation that can be used to predict the concession-stand profit P from the probability of rain R.

2. Use this equation to predict the profit when the probability of rain is 25%. Compare your answer with your result in Question A, part (1).

C. **1.** Write an equivalent expression for the profit in Question B. Explain why the two expressions are equivalent.

2. Predict the probability of rain on a day when the concession-stand profit is \$625. Compare your answer with the result you found in Question A, part (2).

3. Predict the profit when the probability of rain is 0%. Does your answer make sense? Explain.

4. Predict the profit when the probability of rain is 100%. Does your answer make sense?

D. Do the equations in Questions B and C represent a linear, exponential, or quadratic relationship, or none of these? Explain.

ACE **Homework starts on page 28.**

2.3 Area and Profit—What's the Connection?

In the next problem, you will explore two familiar situations that have an interesting connection.

Tony and Paco will operate the water tube concession stand at Water City. Tony is responsible for designing the building that will store the rafts. Paco is responsible for deciding the rental fee for the tubes.

Problem 2.3 Using Equations

A. Every concession stand must have a rectangular floor space and a perimeter of 88 meters. Tony wants the greatest area possible.

1. Write an equation for the area in terms of the length.
2. What is the maximum area for the rectangular floor space?

B. Paco knows that on a typical day, the number of tube rentals n is related to the price to rent each tube p. Records from other water park locations suggest:

- If the tubes are free (no price), there will be 54 rentals.
- Each increase of \$1 in the price will result in one less tube rented.

Paco uses this information to write the following equations:

- Equation 1: $n = 54 - (1)p$
- Equation 2: $I = np$, where I is the daily income

1. Do these equations make sense? Explain.
2. Write an equation for income in terms of the number of rentals n.
3. The expenses for storage and maintenance of the rented tubes are \$10 per day. Write an equation for daily profit D in terms of the number of rentals n.

4. Compare the equation in part (3) to the equation in Question A, part (1).

5. What number of rentals produces the maximum daily profit? What is the maximum profit? What rental price produces the maximum daily profit?

ACE **Homework starts on page 28.**

Did You Know?

The calculation of the quarterback rating in the National Football League (NFL™) uses a series of equations:

$$\text{Completion Rating: CR} = 5\left(\frac{\text{completions}}{\text{attempts}}\right) - 1.5$$

$$\text{Yards Rating: YR} = \frac{\frac{\text{yards}}{\text{attempts}} - 3}{4}$$

$$\text{Touchdown Rating: TR} = 20\left(\frac{\text{touchdowns}}{\text{attempts}}\right)$$

$$\text{Interception Rating: IR} = 25\left(0.095 - \frac{\text{interceptions}}{\text{attempts}}\right)$$

$$\text{Overall Rating} = 100\left(\frac{\text{CR} + \text{YR} + \text{TR} + \text{IR}}{6}\right)$$

For: Information about quarterback ratings
Web Code: ape-9031

Applications

Connections

Extensions

Applications

1. The student council is organizing a T-shirt sale to raise money for a local charity. They make the following estimates of expenses and income:

- Expense of \$250 for advertising
- Expense of \$4.25 for each T-shirt
- Income of \$12 for each T-shirt
- Income of \$150 from a business sponsor

a. Write an equation for the income I made for selling n T-shirts.

b. Write an equation for the expenses E for selling n T-shirts.

c. Suppose the student council sells 100 T-shirts. What is the profit?

d. Write an equation for the profit P made for selling n T-shirts.

For Exercises 2–5, use the following information: In *Variables and Patterns*, several students were planning a bike tour. They estimated the following expenses and incomes.

- \$30 for each bike rental
- \$125 for cost of food and camp for each biker
- \$700 for van rental
- \$350 of income for each biker

2. a. Write an equation for the total expenses E for n bikers.

b. Write an equation for the total income I for n bikers.

c. Write an equation for the profit P for n bikers.

d. Find the profit for 25 bikers.

e. Suppose the profit is \$1,055. How many bikers went on the trip?

f. Does the profit equation represent a linear, quadratic, or exponential function, or none of these? Explain.

3. Multiple Choice Suppose someone donates a van at no charge. Which equation represents the total expenses?

A. $E = 125 + 30$ **B.** $E = 125n + 30n$

C. $E = 155$ **D.** $E = 155 + n$

Applications

4. **Multiple Choice** Suppose people supply their own bikes. Which equation represents the total expenses? (Assume they will rent a van.)

F. $E = 125n + 700$ **G.** $E = 125 + 700 + n$

H. $E = 825n$ **J.** $E = 350n + 125n + 700$

5. **Multiple Choice** Suppose people supply their own bikes. Which equation represents the profit? (Assume they will rent a van.)

A. $P = 350 - (125 + 700 + n)$ **B.** $P = 350n - 125n + 700$

C. $P = 350n - (125n + 700)$ **D.** $P = 350 - 125n - 700$

For Exercises 6–8, recall the equations from Problem 2.2 ($P = 2.50V - 500$ and $V = 600 - 500R$).

6. Suppose the probability of rain is 50%. What profit can the concession stand expect to make?

7. What is the probability of rain if the profit expected is $100?

8. The manager estimates the daily employee-bonus fund B (in dollars) from the number of visitors V using the equation $B = 100 + 0.50V$.

   a. Suppose the probability of rain is 30%. What is the daily employee-bonus fund?

   b. Write an equation that relates the employee-bonus B to the probability of rain R.

   c. Suppose the probability of rain is 50%. Use your equation to calculate the employee-bonus fund.

   d. Suppose the daily employee-bonus fund is $375. What is the probability of rain?

For: Help with Exercise 8
Web Code: ape-6208

9. A manager of a park claims that the profit P for a concession stand depends on the number of visitors V, and that the number of visitors depends on the day's high temperature T (in Fahrenheit). The following equations represent the manager's claims:

$$P = 4.25V - 300 \qquad V = 50(T - 45)$$

a. Suppose 1,000 people visit the park one day. Predict that day's high temperature.

b. Write an equation for profit based on temperature.

c. Write an equation for profit that is equivalent to the equation in part (b). Explain what information the numbers and variables represent.

d. Find the profit if the temperature is 70°F.

10. A farmer has 240 meters of fence. The farmer wants to build a fence to enclose the greatest possible rectangular land area.

a. Write an equation for the fenced area A in terms of the length ℓ of the rectangular plot.

b. What are the dimensions of the rectangle with the greatest area?

c. Describe how you could find the information in part (b) from a graph of the equation.

d. Does the equation for area represent a linear, quadratic, or exponential function, or none of these? Explain.

11. In Exercise 10, suppose the farmer uses the 240 meters of fence to enclose a rectangular plot on only three sides and uses a creek as the boundary of the fourth side.

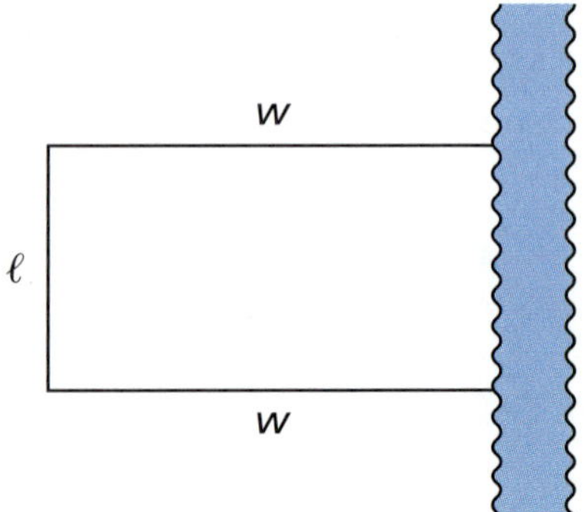

a. Write an equation for the fenced area A in terms of the length ℓ of the rectangular plot.

b. What are the dimensions of the rectangle with the greatest area?

c. Does the equation represent a linear, quadratic, or exponential function, or none of these? Explain.

12. The math club is selling posters to advertise National Algebra day. The following equation represents the profits P they expect for selling n posters at x dollars.

$$P = xn - 6n$$

They also know that the number of posters n sold depends on the selling price x, which is represented by this equation:

$$n = 20 - x$$

   a. Write an equation for profit in terms of the number of posters sold. **Hint:** First solve the equation $n = 20 - x$ for x.

   b. What is the profit for selling 10 posters?

   c. What is the selling price of the posters in part (b)?

   d. What is the greatest possible profit?

Connections

13. **Multiple Choice** Which statement is *false* when a, b, and c are different real numbers?

   F. $(a + b) + c = a + (b + c)$ **G.** $ab = ba$

   H. $(ab)c = a(bc)$ **J.** $a - b = b - a$

For Exercises 14–16, use the Distributive Property and sketch a rectangle to show the equivalence.

14. $x(x + 5)$ and $x^2 + 5x$

15. $(2 + x)(2 + 3x)$ and $4 + 8x + 3x^2$

16. $(x + 2)(2x + 3)$ and $2x^2 + 7x + 6$

For: Multiple-Choice Skills Practice
Web Code: apa-6254

17. Some steps are missing in the solution to $11x - 12 = 30 + 5x$.

$$11x - 12 = 30 + 5x$$
$$11x = 42 + 5x$$
$$6x = 42$$
$$x = 7$$

   a. Copy the steps above. Fill in the missing steps.

   b. How can you check that $x = 7$ is the correct solution?

   c. Explain how you could use a graph or a table to solve the original equation for x.

18. In the following graph, line ℓ_1 represents the income for selling n soccer balls. Line ℓ_2 represents the expenses of manufacturing n soccer balls.

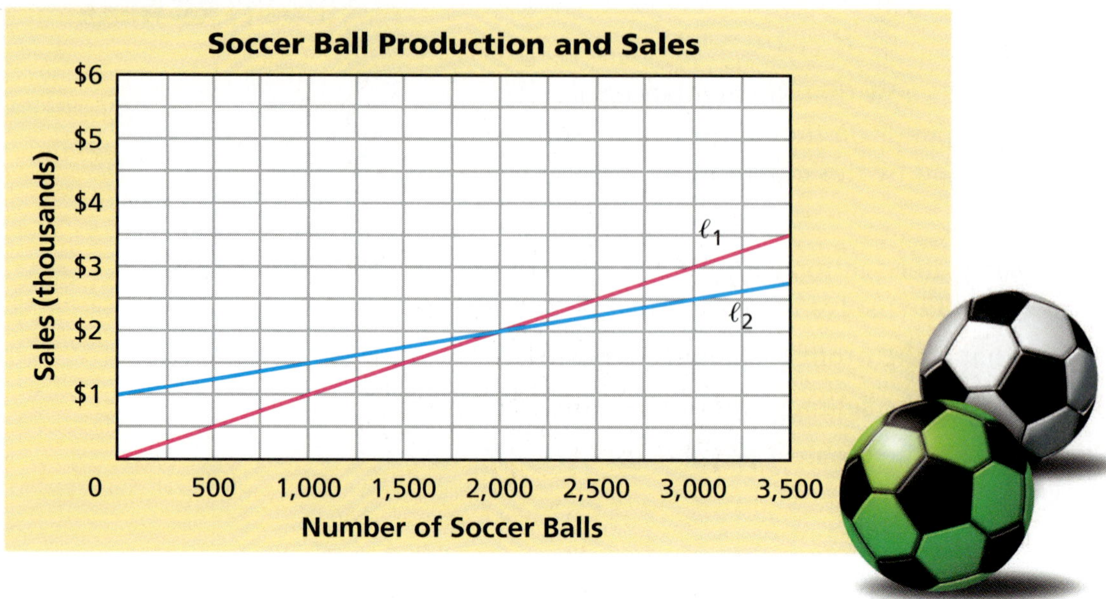

a. What is the start-up expense (the expense before any soccer balls are produced) for manufacturing the soccer balls? NOTE: The vertical axis is in *thousands* of dollars.

b. What are the expenses and income for producing and selling 500 balls? For 1,000 balls? For 3,000 balls? Explain.

c. What is the profit for producing and selling 500 balls? For 1,000 balls? For 3,000 balls? Explain.

d. What is the break-even point? Give the number of soccer balls and the expenses.

e. Write equations for the expenses, income, and profit. Explain what the numbers and variables in each equation represent.

f. Suppose the manufacturer produces and sells 1,750 soccer balls. Use the equations in part (e) to find the profit.

g. Suppose the profit is $10,000. Use the equations in part (e) to find the number of soccer balls produced and sold.

For Exercises 19–24, use properties of equality to solve the equation. Check your solution.

19. $7x + 15 = 12x + 5$

20. $7x + 15 = 5 + 12x$

21. $-3x + 5 = 2x - 10$

22. $14 - 3x = 1.5x + 5$

23. $9 - 4x = \frac{3 + x}{2}$

24. $-3(x + 5) = \frac{2x - 10}{3}$

25. The writing club wants to publish a book of students' short stories, poems, and essays. A member of the club contacts two local printers to get bids on the cost of printing the books.

Bid 1: cost = \$100 + \$4 × the number of books printed

Bid 2: cost = \$25 + \$7 × the number of books printed

a. Make a table of (*number of books printed*, *cost*) values for each bid. Use your table to find the number of books for which the two bids are equal. Explain how you found your answer.

b. Make a graph of the two equations. Use your graph to find the number of books for which the two bids are equal. Explain.

c. For what numbers of books is Bid 1 less than Bid 2? Explain.

26. Use the information about printing costs from Exercise 25.

a. For each bid, find the cost of printing 75 books.

b. Suppose the cost cannot exceed \$300. For each bid, find the greatest number of books that can be printed. Explain.

The club decides to request bids from two more printers.

Bid 3: cost = \$8 × the number of books printed

Bid 4: cost = \$30 + \$6 × the number of books printed

c. For what number of books does Bid 3 equal Bid 4? Explain.

27. a. A soccer team has 21 players. Suppose each player shakes hands with each of the other players. How many handshakes will take place?

b. Write an equation for the number of handshakes h among a team with n players.

c. Write an equation for the number of handshakes that is equivalent to the equation in part (b).

Connections

28. **a.** Write an expression that is equivalent to $(x + 2)(x + 5)$.

b. Explain two methods for checking equivalence.

29. For the equation $y = (x + 2)(x + 5)$, find each of the following. Explain how you found each.

a. y-intercept

b. x-intercept(s)

c. maximum/minimum point

d. line of symmetry

For Exercises 30–35, find an equivalent expression.

30. $x^2 \cdot x^3$

31. $x \cdot x^0 \cdot x^5$

32. $\frac{x^2 \cdot x^3}{x}$

33. $\frac{x^8}{x^5}$

34. $\frac{x^5}{x^8}$

35. $\frac{4x^8}{2x^5}$

36. Mary's salary is $30,000 per year. What would be her new salary next year given each condition?

a. She gets a 15% raise.

b. Her salary grows by a factor of 1.12.

c. Her salary increases to 110% of what it is now.

37. Examine the three different cylinders.

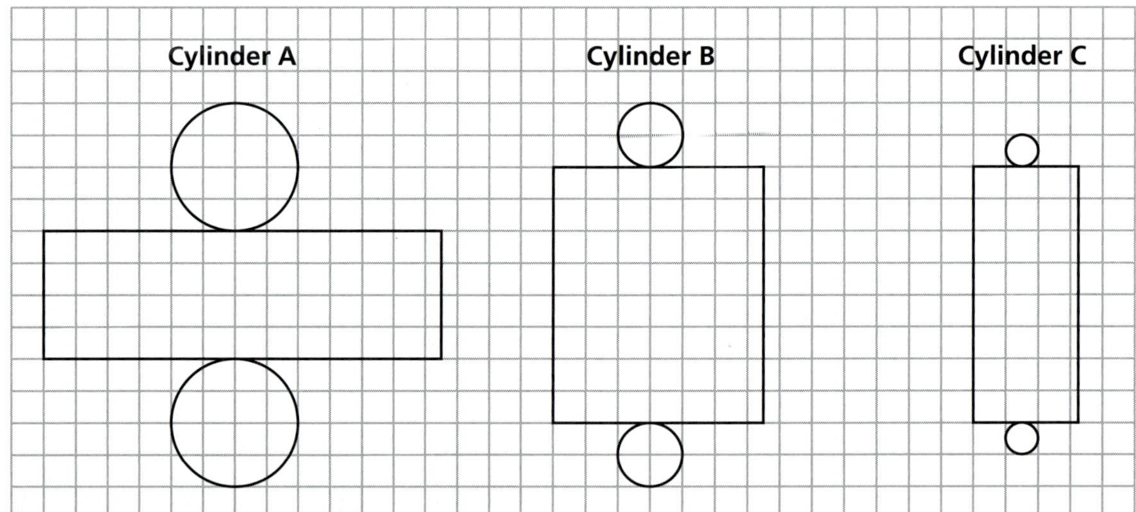

a. Compare the three cylinders.

b. Estimate the surface area of each cylinder. Which cylinder has the greatest surface area? Explain.

c. Which cylinder has the greatest volume? Explain.

Extensions

38. The Phillips Concert Hall estimates their concession-stand profits P_c and admission profits P_A with the following equations, where x is the number of people (in hundreds):

$$P_c = 15x - 500 \qquad P_A = 106x - x^2$$

The concession-stand profits include revenue from advertising and the sale of food and souvenirs. The admission profits are based on the difference between ticket sales and cost.

a. Write an equation for the total profit for P in terms of the number of people x (in hundreds).

b. What is the maximum profit? How many people must attend in order to achieve the maximum profit?

39. Recall the series of equations used to calculate a quarterback's rating in the *Did You Know?* after Problem 2.3. Tom Brady's statistics for 2004 are shown below. Use the equations and the statistics to find his overall rating that year.

Attempts: 474

Completions: 288

Yards: 3,692

Touchdowns: 28

Interceptions: 14

Mathematical Reflections 2

In this investigation, you combined expressions or substituted an equivalent expression for a quantity to make new expressions. You also used these expressions to make predictions. These questions will help you summarize what you have learned.

Think about your answers to these questions. Discuss your ideas with other students and your teacher. Then write a summary of your findings in your notebook.

1. Describe a situation in which it is helpful to add expressions to form a new expression. Explain how you can combine the expressions.
2. Describe a situation in which it is helpful to substitute an equivalent expression for a quantity in an equation.
3. What are the advantages and disadvantages of working with one equation rather than two or more equations in a given situation?

Investigation 

Solving Equations

A problem often requires finding solutions to equations. In previous units, you developed strategies for solving linear and quadratic equations. In this investigation, you will use the properties of real numbers to extend these strategies.

3.1 Solving Linear Equations

How do you solve the following linear equation for x?

$$100 + 4x = 25 + 7x$$

Getting Ready for Problem 3.1

The steps below show one way to solve $100 + 4x = 25 + 7x$.

$$100 + 4x = 25 + 7x$$

(1) $$100 + 4x - 4x = 25 + 7x - 4x$$

$$100 = 25 + 3x$$

(2) $$100 - 25 = 25 + 3x - 25$$

$$75 = 3x$$

(3) $$75 \div 3 = 3x \div 3$$

$$25 = x$$

- Provide an explanation for each numbered step in the solution.
- The solution above begins by subtracting $4x$ from both sides of the equation. Could you begin with a different first step? Explain.
- How can you check that $x = 25$ is the correct solution?
- Describe another method for finding the solution to the equation.

The example in the Getting Ready uses the **properties of equality** that you learned in *Moving Straight Ahead*.

- You can add or subtract the same quantity to both sides of an equation to write an equivalent equation.
- You can multiply or divide both sides of an equation by the same non-zero number to write an equivalent equation.

You will continue to use these properties as well as the Distributive and Commutative properties to solve more equations.

Problem 3.1 Solving Linear Equations

A. A school choir is selling boxes of greeting cards to raise money for a trip.

The equation for the profit in dollars P in terms of the number of boxes sold s is:

$P = 5s - (100 + 2s)$

1. What information do the expressions $5s$ and $100 + 2s$ represent in the situation? What information do 100 and $2s$ represent?

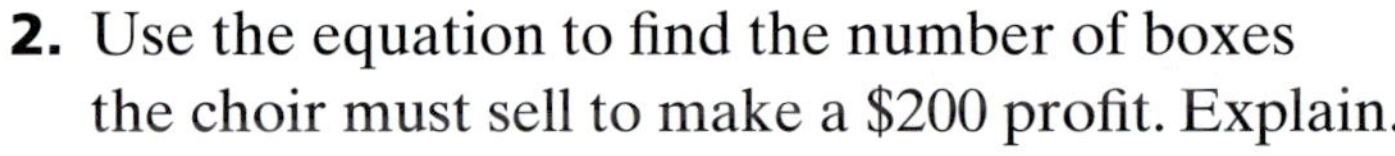

2. Use the equation to find the number of boxes the choir must sell to make a \$200 profit. Explain.
3. How many boxes must the choir sell to break even? Explain.
4. Write a simpler expression for profit. Explain what information the variables and numbers represent.
5. One of the choir members wrote the following expression for profit: $5s - 2(50 + s)$. Explain whether this expression is equivalent to the original expression for profit.

B. Describe how to solve an equation that has parentheses like $200 = 5s - (100 + 2s)$ without using a table or graph.

C. Solve each equation for x when $y = 0$. Check your solutions.

1. $y = 5 + 2(3 + 4x)$
2. $y = 5 - 2(3 + 4x)$
3. $y = 5 + 2(3 - 4x)$
4. $y = 5 - 2(3 - 4x)$

ACE Homework starts on page 45.

3.2 Comparing Costs

Ms. Lucero wants to install tiles around her square swimming pool. She receives two estimates:

- *Cover and Surround It* has a fixed charge of \$1,000 for design and material delivery costs. They charge \$25 per tile after the first 12 tiles.
- *Tile and Beyond* has a fixed charge of \$740 for design and material delivery costs. They charge \$32 per tile after the first 10 tiles.

The equations below show the estimated costs C (in dollars) of buying and installing N border tiles.

Cover and Surround It: $C_C = 1{,}000 + 25(N - 12)$

Tile and Beyond: $C_T = 740 + 32(N - 10)$

Recall that you can use *subscripts* to show different uses for a variable: C_C means cost for *Cover and Surround It*; C_T means cost for *Tile and Beyond*.

- Do the equations make sense given the description above for each company's charges?

Ms. Lucero wants to know when the costs of each company are the same.

How can Ms. Lucero use the equation $C_C = C_T$ to answer her question?

Problem 3.2 Solving More Linear Equations

A. **1.** Without using a table or graph, find the number of tiles for which the two costs are equal.

2. How can you check that your solution is correct?

3. How can you use a graph or table to find the number of tiles for which the two costs are equal?

4. For what numbers of tiles is *Tile and Beyond* cheaper than *Cover and Surround It* ($C_T < C_C$)? Explain your reasoning.

B. Use the techniques that you developed in Problem 3.1 and in Question A to solve each equation for x. Check your solutions.

1. $3x = 5 + 2(3 + 4x)$

2. $10 + 3x = 2(3 + 4x) + 5$

3. $3x = 5 - 2(3 + 4x)$

4. $7 + 3(1 - x) = 5 - 2(3 - 4x)$

ACE Homework starts on page 45.

3.3 Factoring Quadratic Expressions

Sometimes mathematical problems that appear to be different are actually the same. Finding the x-intercepts of $y = x^2 + 5x$ is the same as solving $x^2 + 5x = 0$ for x. The *solutions* to $x^2 + 5x = 0$ are also called the *roots* of the equation. In *Frogs, Fleas, and Painted Cubes* you found the solutions or roots by using a table or graph of $y = x^2 + 5x$ as shown.

x	y	
−7	14	
−6	6	
−5	0	← x-intercept or solution
−4	−4	
−3	−6	
−2	−6	
−1	−4	
0	0	← x-intercept or solution
1	6	
2	14	
3	24	

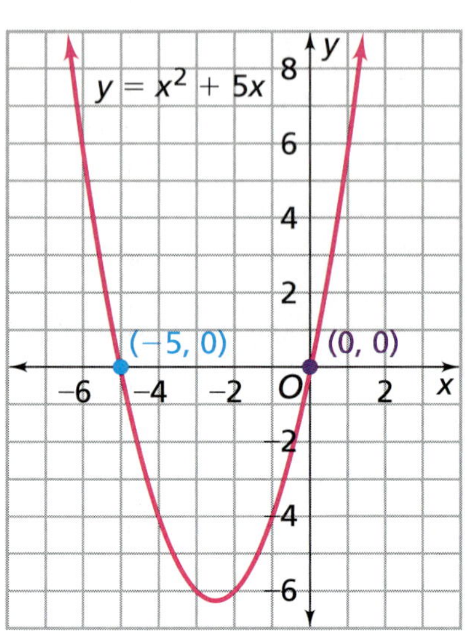

- What is the factored form of $x^2 + 5x$?
- What is the relationship between the factored form of $x^2 + 5x$ and the x-intercepts of the graph of $y = x^2 + 5x$?

Getting Ready for Problem 3.3

To factor the expression $x^2 + 5x + 6$, Trevor draws the area model at the right.

$3x$	6
x^2	$2x$

- Does the model match $x^2 + 5x + 6$?
- Find the factors of $x^2 + 5x + 6$.
- What are the x-intercepts of the graph of $y = x^2 + 5x + 6$?
- Describe the relationship between the x-intercepts of the graph of $y = x^2 + 5x + 6$ and the factored form of $x^2 + 5x + 6$.

Algebra provides tools, such as factoring, that can help solve quadratic equations like $x^2 + 5x = 0$ without using tables or graphs. Before using this tool, you need to review how to write quadratic expressions in factored form.

Problem 3.3 Factoring Quadratic Expressions

A. Jaime suggests the method below to factor $x^2 + 8x + 12$.

- Find factor pairs of 12 such as 1 and 12, 2 and 6, 3 and 4, -1 and -12, -2 and -6, and -3 and -4.
- Pick the factor pair whose sum is 8: $2 + 6 = 8$.
- Write the factored form: $(x + 2)(x + 6)$.

1. Use an area model to show why Jaime's method works for the expression $x^2 + 8x + 12$.

2. Could Jaime have used another factor pair, such as 1 and 12 or 3 and 4, to make an area model for $x^2 + 8x + 12$? Explain.

B. Use a method similar to Jaime's to write each expression in factored form. Show why each factored form is correct.

1. $x^2 + 5x + 4$ **2.** $x^2 - 5x + 4$

3. $x^2 - 3x - 4$ **4.** $x^2 + 4x + 4$

C. 1. Examine the following expressions. How are they similar to and different from those in Question B?

a. $x^2 + 4x$ **b.** $4x^2 + 32x$

c. $6x^2 - 4x$ **d.** $x^2 - 4$

2. Will Jaime's method for factoring work on these expressions? If so, use his method to write them in factored form. If not, find another way to write each in factored form.

D. 1. Examine the following expressions. How are they similar to and different from those in Question B?

a. $2x^2 + 8x + 8$

b. $4x^2 + 4x + 1$

c. $2x^2 + 9x + 4$

2. Will Jaime's method work on these expressions? If so, write them in factored form. If not, find another way to write each in factored form. Explain why your expression is equivalent to the original expression.

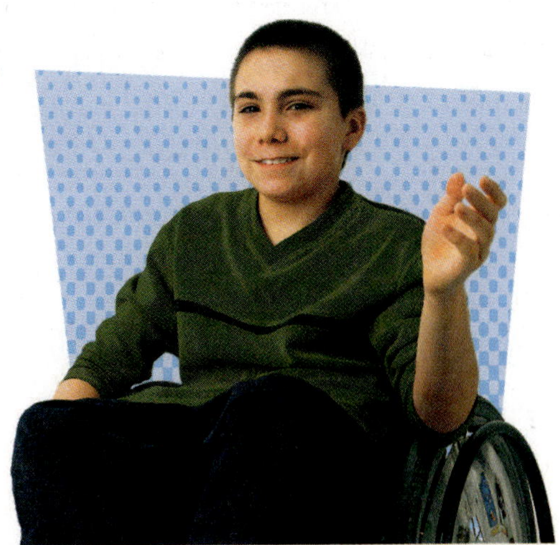

ACE **Homework starts on page 45.**

3.4 Solving Quadratic Equations

In the last problem, you explored ways to write a quadratic expression in factored form. In this problem, you will use the factored form to find solutions to a quadratic equation.

If you know that the product of two numbers is zero, what can you say about the numbers?

Getting Ready for Problem 3.4

- How can you solve the equation $0 = x^2 + 8x + 12$ by factoring?

First write $x^2 + 8x + 12$ in factored form to get $(x + 2)(x + 6)$. This expression is the product of two linear factors.

- When $0 = (x + 2)(x + 6)$, what must be true about one of the linear factors?
- How can this information help you find the solutions to $0 = (x + 2)(x + 6)$?
- How can this information help you find the x-intercepts of $y = x^2 + 8x + 12$?

Problem 3.4 Solving Quadratic Equations

A. **1.** Write $x^2 + 10x + 24$ in factored form.

2. How can you use the factored form to solve $x^2 + 10x + 24 = 0$ for x?

3. Explain how the solutions to $0 = x^2 + 10x + 24$ relate to the graph of $y = x^2 + 10x + 24$.

B. Solve each equation for x without making a table or graph.

1. $0 = (x + 1)(2x + 7)$

2. $0 = (5 - x)(x - 2)$

3. $0 = x^2 + 6x + 9$

4. $0 = x^2 - 16$

5. $0 = x^2 + 10x + 16$

6. $0 = 2x^2 + 7x + 6$

7. How can you check your solutions without using a table or graph?

C. Solve each equation for x without making a table or graph. Check your answers.

1. $0 = x(9 - x)$

2. $0 = -3x(2x + 5)$

3. $0 = 2x^2 + 32x$

4. $0 = 18x - 9x^2$

D. You can approximate the height h of a pole-vaulter from the ground after t seconds with the equation $h = 32t - 16t^2$.

1. Suppose the pole-vaulter writes the equation $0 = 32t - 16t^2$. What information is the pole-vaulter looking for?

2. The pole-vaulter wants to clear a height of 17.5 feet. Will the pole-vaulter clear the desired height? Explain.

ACE **Homework starts on page 45.**

You can find the solutions to many quadratic equations using tables or graphs. Sometimes, however, these methods will give only approximate answers. For example, the solutions to the equation $x^2 - 2 = 0$ are $x = \sqrt{2}$ and $x = -\sqrt{2}$. Using a table or graph, you only get an approximation for $\sqrt{2}$.

You can try a factoring method, but the probability of readily factoring any quadratic expression $ax^2 + bx + c$, where a, b, and c are real numbers is small.

We know that the Greeks used a geometric method to solve quadratic equations around 300 B.C. Mathematicians from India probably had methods for solving these equations around 500 B.C., but their methods remain unknown.

For years, mathematicians tried to find a general solution to $ax^2 + bx + c = 0$. In a book published in 1591, François Viète was the first person to develop a formula for finding the roots of a quadratic equation. It is called the *quadratic formula* and is given below.

$$x = \frac{-b \pm \sqrt{b^2 - 4ac}}{2a}$$

This formula can be used for any quadratic equation. You will learn more about this formula in later mathematics courses.

For: Information about François Viète
Web Code: ape-9031

Applications Connections Extensions

Applications

1. The organizers of a walkathon discuss expenses and income. They make the following estimates:

- Expense for advertisement: \$500
- Expense for participant T-shirts: \$6 per child, \$8.50 per adult
- Income from business sponsors: \$1,000
- Expense for emergency medical services: \$250
- Income from registration fees: \$5 per child, \$15 per adult

a. Suppose 30 adults and 40 children participate in the walkathon. Find the total income, the total expenses, and the profit. Show your work.

b. Write an equation showing the profit P in the form:

P = (expression for income) − (expression for expenses).

c. Write another expression for profit that is equivalent to the one in part (b).

d. Suppose 30 adults and 40 children participate. Use your equation from part (b) or part (c) to find the profit. Compare your answer to the profit you calculated in part (a).

e. Suppose 100 children participate and the profit is \$1,099. How many adults participated? Show your work.

2. Marcel and Kirsten each try to simplify the following equation:
$P = (1{,}000 + 5c + 15a) - (500 + 6c + 8.50a + 250)$

They are both incorrect. Study the steps in their reasoning and identify their mistakes.

a.

Marcel

$$\begin{aligned} P &= (1{,}000 + 5c + 15a) - (500 + 6c + 8.50a + 250) \\ &= 1{,}000 + 5c + 15a - 500 + 6c + 8.50a + 250 \\ &= 1{,}000 - 500 + 250 + 5c + 6c + 15a + 8.50a \\ &= 750 + 11c + 23.50a \quad \textit{incorrect answer} \end{aligned}$$

b.

Kirsten

$$\begin{aligned} P &= (1{,}000 + 5c + 15a) - (500 + 6c + 8.50a + 250) \\ &= 1{,}000 + 5c + 15a - 500 - 6c - 8.50a - 250 \\ &= 1{,}000 - 500 - 250 + 5c - 6c + 15a - 8.50a \\ &= 250 + c + 6.50a \quad \textit{incorrect answer} \end{aligned}$$

3. According to the equation $V = 200 + 50(T - 70)$, the number of visitors to a park depends on the day's high temperature T (in Fahrenheit). Suppose 1,000 people visited the park one day. Predict that day's high temperature.

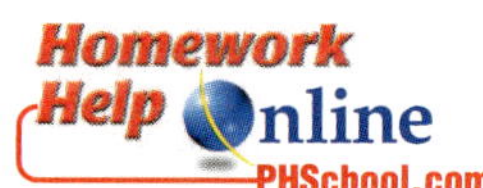

For: Help with Exercise 3
Web Code: ape-6303

For Exercises 4–7, solve each equation for x using the techniques that you developed in Problem 3.1. Check your solutions.

4. $10 + 2(3 + 2x) = 0$

5. $10 - 2(3 + 2x) = 0$

6. $10 + 2(3 - 2x) = 0$

7. $10 - 2(3 - 2x) = 0$

8. The two companies from Problem 3.2 decide to lower their costs for a Fourth of July sale. The equations below show the lower estimated costs C (in dollars) of buying and installing N border tiles.

Cover and Surround It: $C_C = 750 + 22(N - 12)$

Tile and Beyond: $C_T = 650 + 30(N - 10)$

a. Without using a table or graph, find the number of tiles for which the cost estimates from the two companies are equal.

b. How can you check that your solution is correct?

c. Explain how a graph or table could be used to find the number of tiles for which the costs are equal.

d. For what numbers of tiles is *Tile and Beyond* cheaper than *Cover and Surround It*? Explain your reasoning.

e. Write another expression that is equivalent to the expression for *Tile and Beyond's* cost estimate (C_T). Explain what information the variables and numbers represent.

9. The school choir from Problem 3.1 has the profit plan $P = 5s - (100 + 2s)$. The school band also sells greeting cards. The equation for the band's profit is $P = 4s - 2(10 + s)$. Find the number of boxes that each group must sell to have equal profits.

For Exercises 10–17, solve each equation for x without using tables or graphs. Check your solutions.

10. $8x + 16 = 6x$

11. $8(x + 2) = 6x$

12. $6 + 8(x + 2) = 6x$

13. $4 + 5(x + 2) = 7x$

14. $2x - 3(x + 6) = -4(x - 1)$

15. $2 - 3(x + 4) = 9 - (3 + 2x)$

16. $2.75 - 7.75(5 - 2x) = 26$

17. $\frac{1}{2}x + 4 = \frac{2}{3}x$

18. Write each product in expanded form.

a. $(x - 2)(x + 2)$

b. $(x - 5)(x + 5)$

c. $(x - 4)(x + 4)$

d. $(x - 12)(x + 12)$

19. Write each of these quadratic expressions in equivalent factored form.

a. $x^2 + 5x + 4$

b. $8 + x^2 + 6x$

c. $x^2 - 7x + 10$

d. $x^2 + 7x$

e. $x^2 - 6 + 5x$

f. $2x^2 - 5x - 12$

g. $x^2 - 7x - 8$

h. $x^2 - 5x$

Go Online PHSchool.com
For: Multiple-Choice Skills Practice
Web Code: apa-6354

20. Write each of these expressions in factored form.

a. $x^2 - 16$

b. $x^2 - 36$

c. $x^2 - 49$

d. $x^2 - 400$

e. $x^2 - 64$

f. $x^2 - 144$

For Exercises 21–23, solve each equation for *x*. Check your solutions by using calculator tables or graphs.

21. $x^2 + 1.5x = 0$

22. $x^2 + 6x + 8 = 0$

23. $8x - x^2 = 0$

24. The equation $H = -16t^2 + 8t$ describes the height of a flea (in feet) after t seconds during a jump.

a. Is the flea's jump equation linear, quadratic, or exponential?

b. Write an expression that is equivalent to $-16t^2 + 8t$.

c. Without using a graph or a table, find the time when the flea lands on the ground. Explain how you found your answer.

25. Use an area model to factor each expression.

a. $x^2 + 8x + 15$

b. $x^2 - 9$

c. $2x^2 + 5x + 3$

26. Use your answers to Exercise 25 to solve each equation.

a. $x^2 + 8x + 15 = 0$

b. $x^2 - 9 = 0$

c. $2x^2 + 5x + 3 = 0$

In Exercises 27 and 28, each solution contains an error.

- Find the error, and correct the solution.
- How would you help a student who made this error?

27.

$6x^2 - x = 1$

Solution

$6x^2 - x - 1 = 0$

$(3x - 1)(2x + 1) = 0$

$3x - 1 = 0$ or $2x + 1 = 0$

$x = \frac{1}{3}$ or $x = -\frac{1}{2}$

incorrect answer

28.

$24n^2 - 16n = 0$

Solution

$24n^2 - 16n = 0$

$24n^2 = 16n$

$n = \frac{16}{24}$ or $n = \frac{2}{3}$

partially correct answer

Applications | Connections

Connections

29. In Problem 3.1, the equation for profit P in terms of the number of boxes sold s is $P = 5s - (100 + 2s)$. The number of boxes sold also depends on the number of choir members.

a. Suppose each member sells 11 boxes. Write an equation that will predict profit from the number of choir members n.
Hint: First find an expression for the number of boxes sold.

b. Write an equivalent expression for profit in part (a). Explain what the variables and numbers represent.

c. Suppose the choir has 47 members. What is the profit?

d. Suppose the profit is \$1,088. How many choir members are there?

e. In part (d), how many boxes were sold?

30. The equations $N = 2s + 2(s + 2)$ and $N = 4(s + 2) - 4$ both represent the number of 1-foot square border tiles needed to surround a square pool with sides of length s in feet.

a. Suppose $N = 48$. Solve $N = 2s + 2(s + 2)$ for s.

b. Suppose $N = 48$. Solve $N = 4(s + 2) - 4$ for s.

c. How do your answers for parts (a) and (b) compare? Explain.

31. Multiple Choice If $\frac{3}{4}(x - 4) = 12$, what is the value of x?

A. 6 **B.** 8 **C.** $18\frac{1}{3}$ **D.** 20

32. Multiple Choice What is the value of $x^2(7 - x) + 1$ when $x = 5$?

F. 201 **G.** 28 **H.** 51 **J.** 75

33. In Problem 3.2, you found the number of tiles for which the cost estimates for the two companies were equal. What is the side length of the largest square pool that can be surrounded by that number of tiles? Explain your reasoning.

For Exercises 34 and 35, use the Distributive and Commutative properties to simplify each expression. Check that the original expression and your simplified expression are equivalent by testing several *x* values in both expressions.

34. $2(9x + 15) - (8 + 2x)$ **35.** $(7x - 12) - 2(3x + 10)$

Each figure in Exercises 36–40 has an area of 24 square meters. Find each labeled dimension.

36.

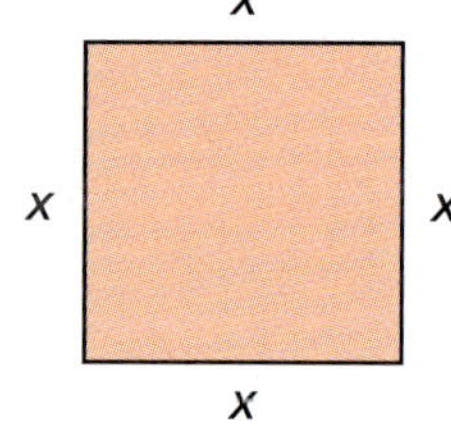

37.

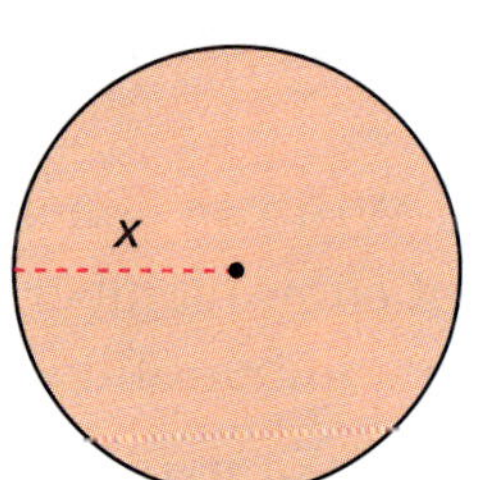

38.

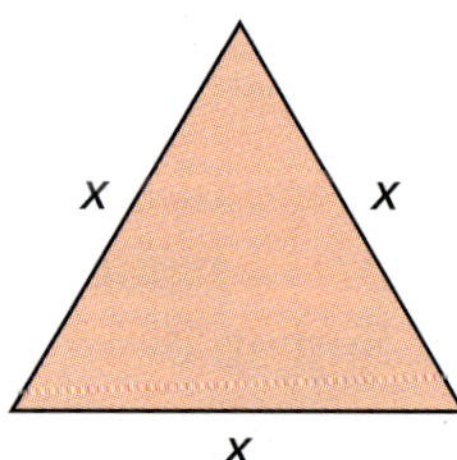

39.

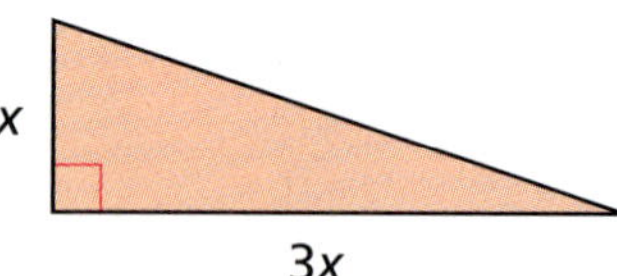

40.

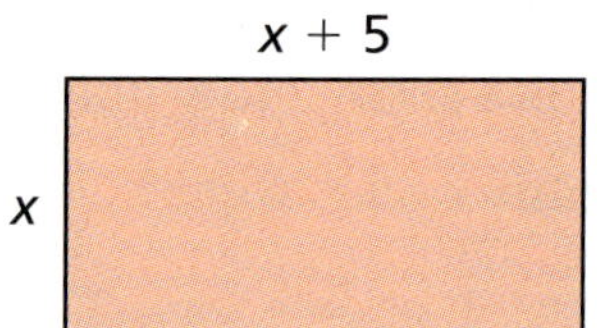

41. An oil company ships oil in spherical tanks that are 3 meters in diameter. The company now wants to ship oil in cylindrical tanks that are 4 meters high, but have the same volume as the spheres. What radius must the cylindrical tanks have?

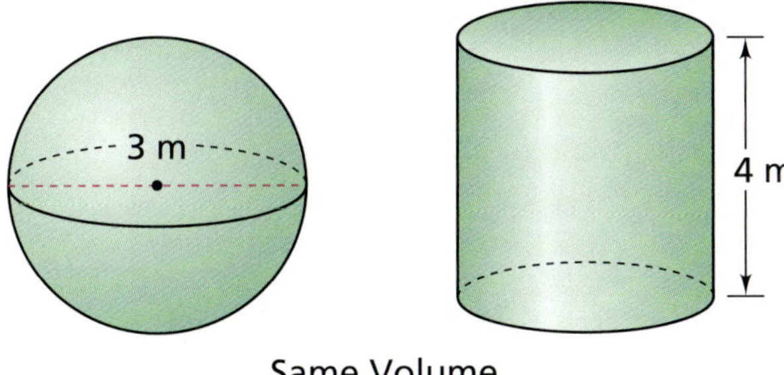

Same Volume
Not drawn to scale

42. Write a quadratic equation that has

a. one solution (one x-intercept)

b. two solutions (two x-intercepts)

43. John wants to know if he can bounce a superball over his house. You can approximate the height h of the superball on one bounce with the equation $h = 48t - 16t^2$, where t is the number of seconds after the ball hits the ground.

a. How long is the ball in the air?

b. Suppose his house is 30 feet tall. Will the ball make it over his house? Explain.

44. You can write quadratic expressions in factored and expanded forms. Which form would you use for each of the following? Explain.

a. to determine whether a quadratic relationship has a maximum point or a minimum point

b. to find the x- and y-intercepts of a quadratic relationship

c. to find the line of symmetry for a quadratic relationship

d. to find the coordinates of the maximum or minimum point for a quadratic relationship

Connections

45. Each team in a lacrosse league must play each of the other teams. The number of games g played in a league with n teams is $g = n^2 - n$. What are the x-intercepts for the graph of this equation? Explain what information they represent.

46. The height (in feet) of an arch above a point x feet from one of its bases is approximated by the equation $y = 0.2x(1{,}000 - x)$. What is the maximum height of the arch? Explain.

Extensions

For Exercises 47 and 48, find the value of c for which $x = 3$ is the solution to the equation.

47. $3x + c = 2x - 2c$

48. $3x + c = cx - 2$

49. Write two linear equations that have the solution $x = 3$. Are there more than two equations with a solution of $x = 3$? Explain.

50. Insert parentheses into the expression $13 = 3 + 5x - 2 - 2x + 5$ so that the solution to the equation is $x = 1$.

51. Write the following in expanded form.

a. $(x - .2)(x + .2)$

b. $(x - 12.5)(x + 12.5)$

c. $(x - \sqrt{5})(x + \sqrt{5})$

d. $(x - \sqrt{2})(x + \sqrt{2})$

52. Factor.

a. $x^2 - 100$

b. $x^2 - 1.44$

c. $x^2 - 7$

d. $x^2 - 24$

53. Below are the graphs of $y = 1.5x + 6$ and $y = -2x + 15$. The scale on the x-axis is 1, and the scale on the y-axis is 3.

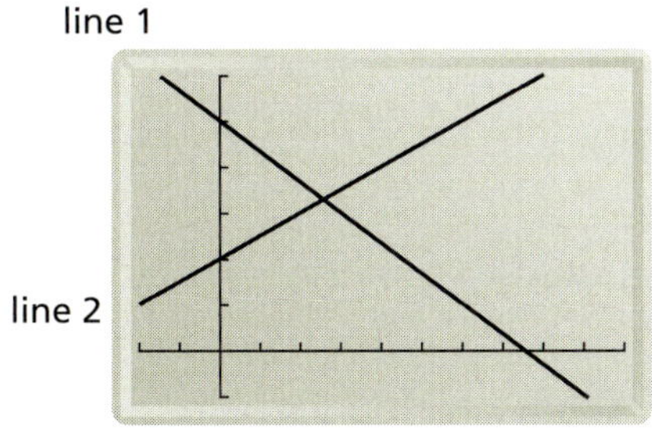

a. Is $y = 1.5x + 6$ or $y = -2x + 15$ the equation of line 1?

b. Find the coordinates of the point of intersection of the two lines.

c. How could you find the answer to part (b) without using a graph or a table?

d. What values of x satisfy the inequality $1.5x + 6 < -2x + 15$? How is your answer shown on the graph?

e. What values of x satisfy the inequality $1.5x + 6 > -2x + 15$? How is your answer shown on the graph?

Connections Extensions

54. Use the graph of $y = x^2 - 9x$ below. The scale on the x-axis is 1. The scale on the y-axis is 2.

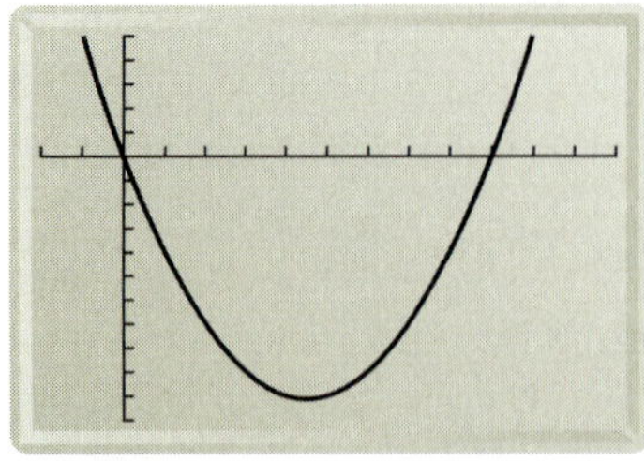

a. What are the coordinates of the x-intercepts?

b. How could you find the answer to part (a) without using a graph or a table?

c. What values of x satisfy the inequality $x^2 - 9x < 0$? How is your answer shown on the graph?

d. What values of x satisfy the inequality $x^2 - 9x > 0$? How is your answer shown on the graph?

e. What is the minimum y-value? What x-value corresponds to this minimum y-value?

55. Use the quadratic formula from the *Did You Know?* after Problem 3.4 to solve each equation.

a. $x^2 - 6x + 8 = 0$

b. $-x^2 - x + 6 = 0$

c. $10 - 7x + x^2 = 0$

d. $4x^2 - x = 0$

e. $2x^2 - 12x + 18 = 0$

f. $3x + x^2 - 4 = 0$

For Exercises 56 and 57, use what you have learned in this investigation to solve the equation. Show your work and check your solutions.

56. $x^2 + 5x + 7 = 1$

57. $x^2 + 6x + 15 = 6$

Mathematical Reflections 3

In this investigation, you learned methods for solving linear and quadratic equations. These questions will help you summarize what you have learned.

Think about your answers to these questions. Discuss your ideas with other students and your teacher. Then write a summary of your findings in your notebook.

1. Describe some general strategies for solving linear equations, including those with parentheses. Give examples that illustrate your strategies.
2. Describe some strategies for solving quadratic equations of the form $ax^2 + bx + c = 0$. Give examples.
3. How are the solutions of linear and quadratic equations related to graphs of equations?

Investigation 4

Looking Back at Functions

Throughout your work in algebra, you have identified patterns of change between variables as linear, exponential, and quadratic functions. You have used tables, graphs, and equations to represent and reason about these functions. In this unit, you have found that writing equivalent expressions for a quantity or variable can reveal new information about a situation. This investigation will help pull these ideas together.

4.1 Pumping Water

Every winter, Magnolia Middle School empties their pool for cleaning. Ms. Theodora's math class decides to collect data on the amount of water in the pool and how long it takes to empty it. They write an equation to represent the amount of water w (in gallons) in the pool after t hours.

$$w = -250(t - 5)$$

Problem 4.1 Looking at Patterns of Change

A. Answer the following questions. Explain your reasoning.

1. How many gallons of water are pumped out each hour?
2. How long will it take to empty the pool?
3. How many gallons of water are in the pool at the start?

B. 1. Write an expression for the amount of water in the tank after t hours that is equivalent to the original expression.

2. What information does this new expression tell you about the amount of water in the tank?
3. Which expression is more useful in this situation? Explain.

C. **1.** Describe the pattern of change in the relationship between the two variables w and t.

2. Without graphing the equation, describe the shape of the graph. Include as much information as you can.

D. Suppose the equation for the amount of water w (in gallons) in another pool after t hours is $w = -450(2t - 7)$.

1. How many gallons of water are pumped out each hour?

2. How long will it take to empty the pool?

3. How many gallons of water are in the pool at the start?

4. Write an expression that is equivalent to $-450(2t - 7)$. Which expression is more useful? Explain.

ACE **Homework starts on page 60.**

4.2 Generating Patterns

In this problem, you are given two data points for a linear, exponential, and quadratic relationship. You will use these points to find more data points. Then you will write an equation for each relationship.

Problem 4.2 Linear, Exponential, Quadratic

A. The first two rows in a table of numbers are given below. Write four more numbers in each column to make a linear relationship, an exponential relationship, and a quadratic relationship.

Data Points

x	Linear y	Exponential y	Quadratic y
1	1	1	1
2	4	4	4
3	■	■	■
4	■	■	■
5	■	■	■
6	■	■	■

B. Explain why the pattern in each column is correct.

C. **1.** Write an equation for each relationship. Explain what information the variables and numbers represent.

2. Compare your equations with those of your classmates. Do you all have the same equations? Explain.

ACE **Homework starts on page 60.**

4.3 Sorting Functions

In the following problem, a set of equations relating x and y is given. Some of the expressions for y are in factored form, and some are in expanded form.

Which form is easier to use to determine whether a function is linear, exponential, quadratic, or none of these?

Which form is easier to use to determine the x- and y-intercepts, rates of change, and maximum or minimum points of the graph of the function?

Problem 4.3 Sorting Functions

Use the following equations for Questions A–C.

(1) $y = x^2 + 8x + 16$

(2) $y = \frac{1}{3}(3^x)$

(3) $y = 10 - 2x$

(4) $y = 2x^3 + 5$

(5) $y = (x^2 + 1)(x^2 + 3)$

(6) $y = 0.5^x$

(7) $y = 22 - 2x$

(8) $y = \frac{3}{x}$

(9) $y = (x + 4)(x + 4)$

(10) $y = (4x - 3)(x + 1)$

(11) $y = 20x - 4x^2$

(12) $y = x^2$

(13) $y = 3^{x - 1}$

(14) $y = 16 - 2(x + 3)$

(15) $y = 4x^2 - x - 3$

(16) $y = x + \frac{1}{x}$

(17) $y = 4x(5 - x)$

(18) $y = 2(x - 3) + 6(1 - x)$

A. Which equations represent functions that are

1. linear? **2.** exponential? **3.** quadratic?

B. 1. For each function in Question A, find those equations that represent the same function.

2. Without graphing the equation, describe the shape of the graph of those equations in part (1). Give as much detail as possible, including patterns of change, intercepts, and maximum and minimum points.

C. Pick one linear, one quadratic, and one exponential equation. Describe a problem that could be represented by each equation.

ACE **Homework starts on page 60.**

Applications

Connections

Extensions

Applications

1. A pump is used to empty a swimming pool. The equation $w = -275t + 1{,}925$ represents the gallons of water w that remain in the pool t hours after pumping starts.

a. How many gallons of water are pumped out each hour?

b. How much water is in the pool at the start of pumping?

c. Suppose there are 1,100 gallons of water left in the pool. How long has the pump been running?

d. After how many hours will the pool be empty?

e. Write an equation that is equivalent to $w = -275t + 1{,}925$. What information does it tell you about the situation?

f. Without graphing, describe the shape of the graph of the relationship between w and t.

2. A new pump is used to empty the pool in Exercise 1. The equation $w = -275(2t - 7)$ represents the gallons of water w that remain in the pool t hours after pumping starts.

a. How many gallons of water are pumped out each hour?

b. How much water is in the pool at the start of pumping?

c. Suppose there are 1,000 gallons of water left in the pool. How long has the pump been running?

d. After how many hours will the pool be empty?

e. Write an equation that is equivalent to $w = -275(2t - 7)$. What information does it tell you about the situation?

3. A truck has a broken fuel gauge. Luckily, the driver keeps a record of mileage and gas consumption. The driver uses the data to write an equation for the relationship between the number of gallons of gas in the tank g and the number of miles driven m since the last fill-up.

$$g = 25 - \frac{1}{15}m$$

a. How many gallons of gasoline are in a full tank? Explain.

b. Suppose the driver travels 50 miles after filling the tank. How much gas is left?

c. After filling the tank, how many miles can the driver travel before 5 gallons remain?

d. After filling the tank, how many miles can the driver travel before the tank is empty?

e. How many miles does the driver have to travel in order to use 1 gallon of gas? Explain.

f. In the equation, what do the numbers 25 and $\frac{1}{15}$ tell you about the situation?

Applications

4. A middle school pays $2,500 to print 400 copies of the yearbook. They give some free copies to the yearbook advisor and staff and sell the rest to students. The equation below tells how close the school is to paying for the printing bill.

$$y = 2{,}500 - 15(N - 8)$$

Describe what information the numbers and variables represent in this situation.

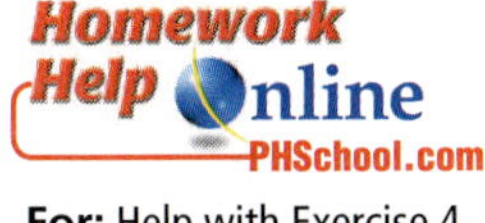

For: Help with Exercise 4
Web Code: ape-6404

5. The Department of Natural Resources is collecting data on three different species of animals. They find that these species show different patterns of population growth. They write the equations below to represent the population P of each species after x years.

Species 1	Species 2	Species 3
$P_1 = 10{,}000 + 100x$	$P_2 = 10(3^x)$	$P_3 = 800 + 10x^2$

a. Describe what information the numbers and variables represent in each equation.

b. Describe the pattern of growth for each species. Explain how the patterns differ.

c. Pick any two species. After how many years will the populations of the two species be equal? Explain how you got your answer.

6. The tables below represent the projected growth of certain species of deer. Use the three tables to answer parts (a)–(c).

Table 1

Year	Deer
2000	1,000
2001	1,030
2002	1,061
2003	1,093
2004	1,126

Table 2

Year	Deer
2000	1,000
2001	1,030
2002	1,060
2003	1,090
2004	1,120

Table 3

Year	Deer
2000	1,000
2001	3,000
2002	9,000
2003	27,000
2004	81,000

a. Describe the growth represented in each table. Are any of these patterns linear, exponential, or quadratic?

b. Write an equation for each linear, exponential, or quadratic pattern in part (a).

c. Does any table show a population of deer growing at a rate of 300% per year? Explain.

7. Suppose the figures shown are made with toothpicks.

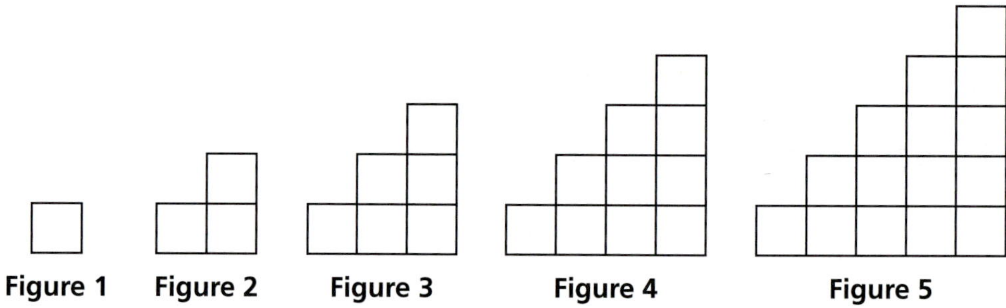

a. What patterns in the set of figures do you notice?

b. How many toothpicks do you need to make Figure 7?

c. Is the relationship between the perimeter and the figure number linear, quadratic, or exponential? Explain.

d. Is the relationship between the total number of toothpicks and the figure number linear, quadratic, or exponential?

e. Write an equation to represent the perimeter of Figure N. Explain your rule.

f. Write an equation to represent the total number of toothpicks needed to make Figure N. Explain your rule.

For Exercises 8–10, use the graphs below.

Graph 1

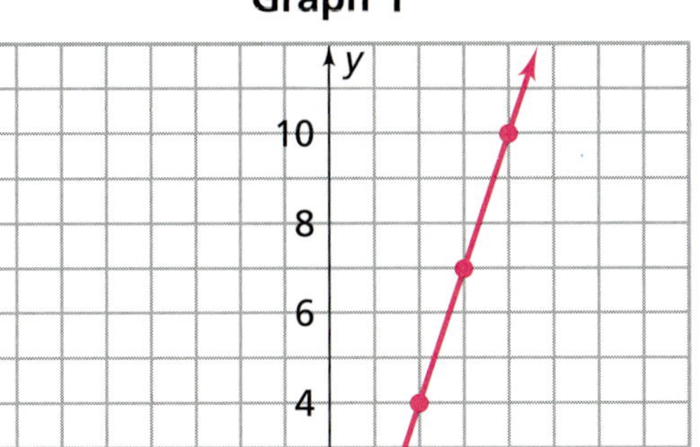

Graph 2

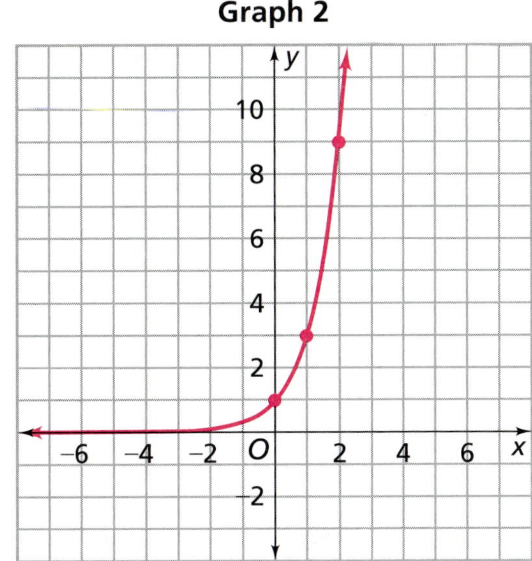

Graph 3

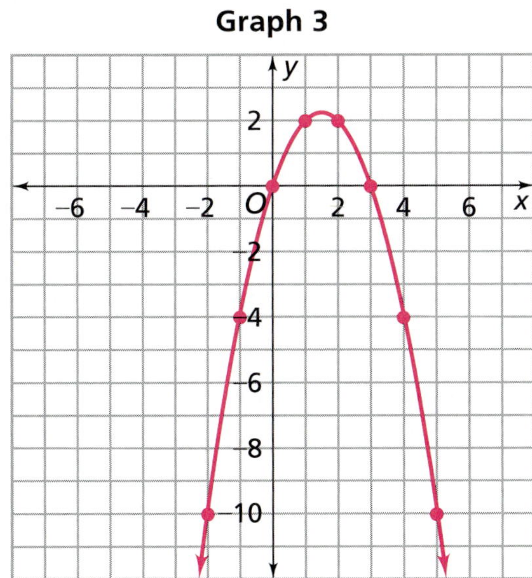

Graph 4

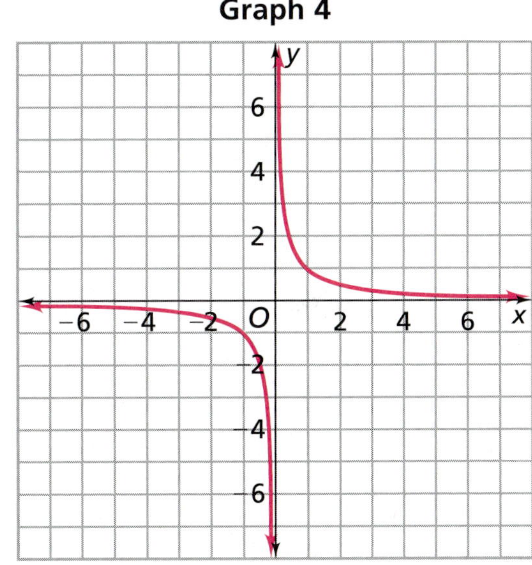

8. Which graphs represent linear, quadratic, or exponential functions?

9. Make a table of y-values for $x = 1, 2, 3, \ldots 6$ for each linear, quadratic, or exponential function.

10. Write an equation for each linear, quadratic, or exponential function. Describe your strategy.

For Exercises 11–17, match each equation with one of the graphs below.

Graph A

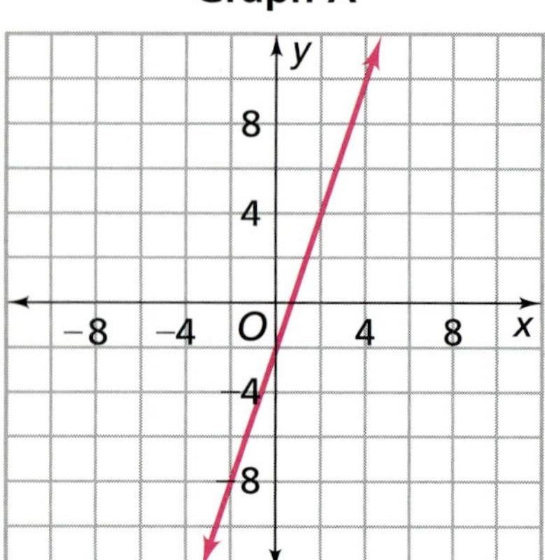

Graph B

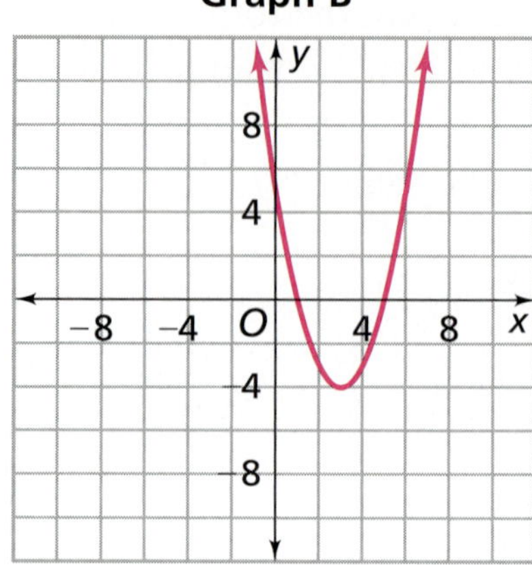

Graph C

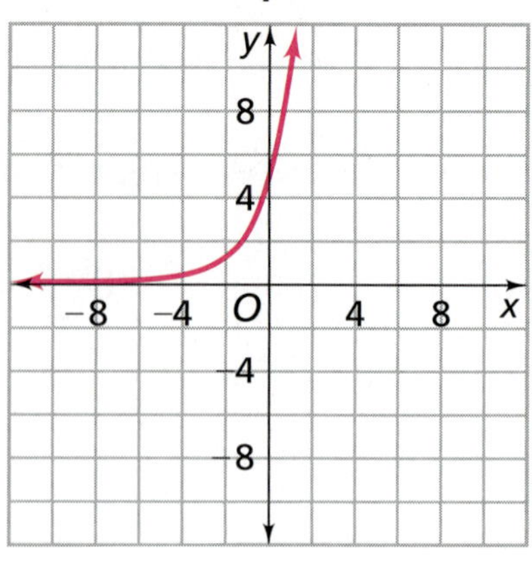

Graph D

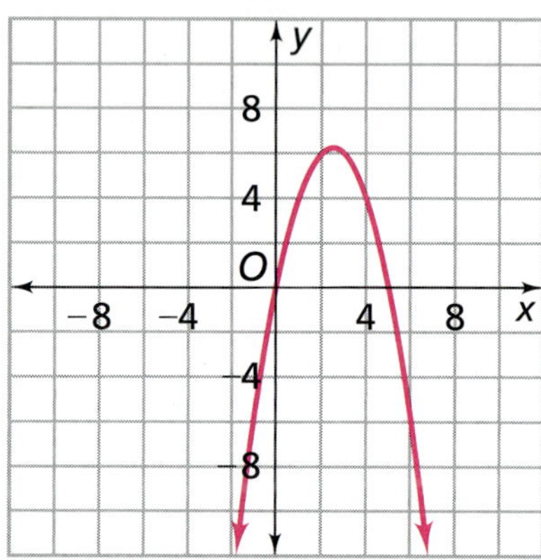

Graph E

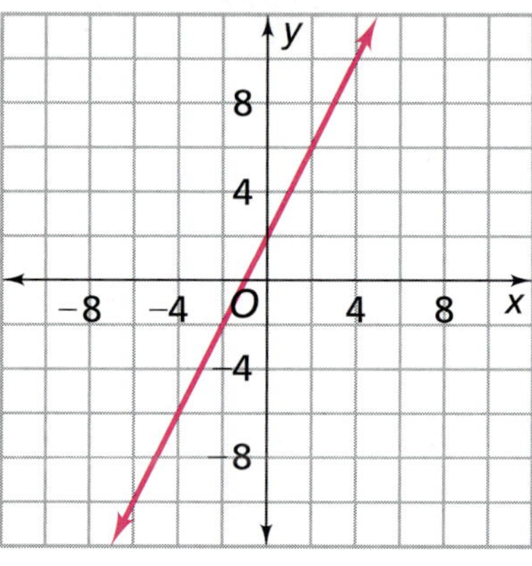

Graph F

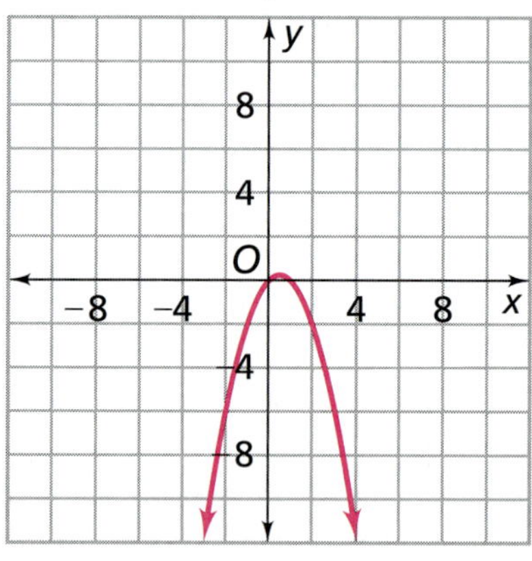

Graph G

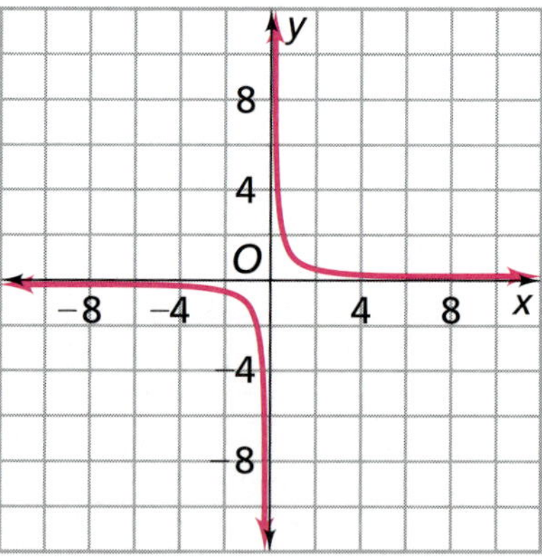

11. $y = \frac{1}{x}$

12. $y = x(5 - x)$

13. $y = (x - 1)(x - 5)$

14. $y = x(1 - x)$

15. $y = 2 + 2x$

16. $y = 5(2^x)$

17. $y = -2 + 3x$

18. For parts (a)–(c), use the set of equations below.

(1) $y = x^2 + 8x$ (4) $y = 2(x - 3) + 6$ (7) $y = 0.25^x$

(2) $y = 2x$ (5) $y = x(x + 8)$ (8) $y = 17 + x(x + 3)$

(3) $y = 4^{x-1}$ (6) $y = 0.25(4^x)$ (9) $y = (x + 1)(x + 17)$

a. Which equations represent linear, quadratic, or exponential functions?

b. Find any equations that represent the same function.

c. Without graphing the equation, describe the shape of the graph of each equation in part (b). Give as much detail as possible, including patterns of change, intercepts, and maximum and minimum points.

19. Pick a linear, quadratic, and exponential equation from Exercise 18. Describe a problem that can be represented by each equation.

Connections

20. Use the figure of the pool for parts (a)–(d). Drawing is not to scale.

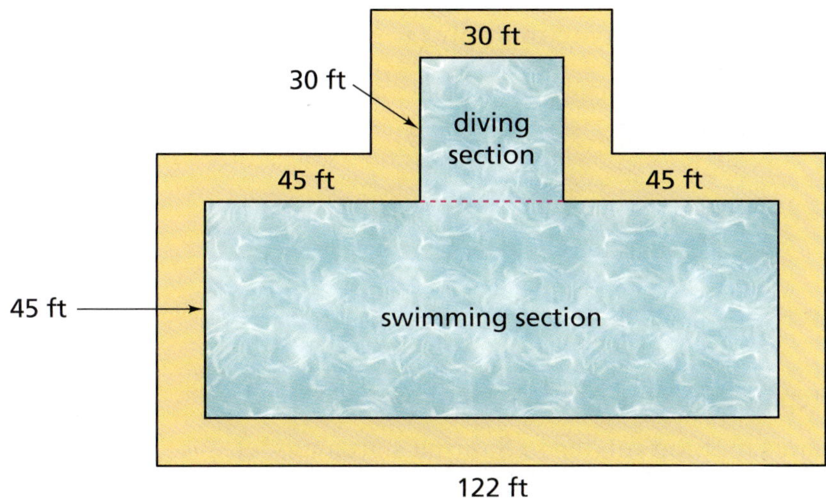

a. How many 1-foot square tiles do you need to build a border that is 1-tile wide around the pool?

b. What is the surface area of the water?

c. The swimming section is 4 feet deep. The diving section is 10 feet deep. What is the volume of the pool?

d. The pool is filled at a rate of 600 cubic feet per hour. How long does it take to fill the pool?

21. **a.** Give the formula for the circumference of a circle with radius r.

b. Give the formula for the area of a circle with radius r.

c. Give the formula for the volume of a cylinder with a height of h and radius of r.

d. For parts (a)–(c), which equations are linear? Explain.

22. A line has a slope of 1.5 and goes through the point $(2, 5)$.

a. Find the coordinates of three other points that lie on the line.

b. Find the coordinates of the y-intercept.

c. Find the y-coordinate of the point whose x-coordinate is -4.

d. Write an equation for the line.

23. Sabrina uses an area model to find the product $(x + 2)(x + 3)$.

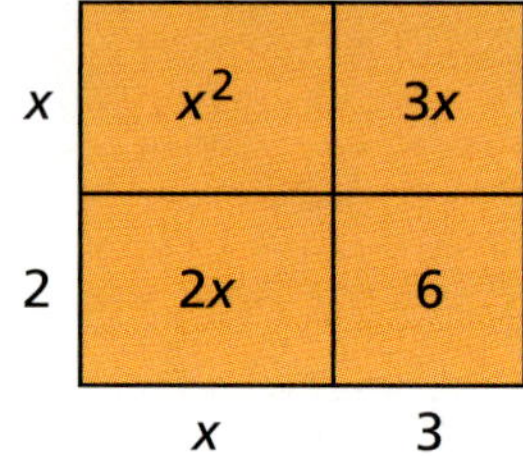

Tara uses the Distributive Property to multiply $(x + 2)(x + 3)$.

$$\begin{aligned}(x + 2)(x + 3) &= (x + 2)x + (x + 2)3 \\ &= x^2 + 2x + 3x + 6 \\ &= x^2 + x(2 + 3) + 6 \\ &= x^2 + 5x + 6\end{aligned}$$

a. Explain each step in Tara's method.

b. Explain how Tara's method relates to Sabrina's area model.

c. Use the Distributive Property to find each product.

i. $(x + 5)(x + 3)$ **ii.** $(x + 4)(x + 1)$ **iii.** $(x - 2)(x + 4)$

Extensions

40. Caley's cell phone company offers two
options for local phone service.

Plan I: $25 for up to 100 minutes, plus

Plan II: $50 for an unlimited number

a. Suppose Caley uses about 200 minut
best option for her? Explain.

b. For what number of minutes are the
Explain.

c. Write an equation for each plan. Des
numbers represent the growth patter

d. Graph each equation on the same co
the graphs describe the growth patte

41. The equation below represents the spac
considered safe given the average veloci
busy street.

$$s = \frac{v^2}{32} + v + $$

a. Suppose a car travels at a rate of 44 f
should it be from the car ahead of it i

b. What is 44 feet per second in miles pe

c. Suppose a taxi is 100 feet behind a ca
for the taxi to be traveling in feet per

24. The equation $d = -16t^2 + 16t + 6.5$ represents the distance d in feet, from the ground to the top of a basketball player's head t seconds after the player jumps.

a. Find the distance to the top of the player's head after 0.1 second.

b. Find the distance to the top of the player's head after 0.3 second.

c. Find the distance to the top of the player's head after 1 second.

d. What operations did you perform to calculate your answers in parts (a)–(c)? In what order did you perform the operations?

25. A bacteria colony begins with 5,000 bacteria. The population doubles every hour. This pattern of exponential growth can be modeled by the equation $b = 5{,}000(2^t)$, where b is the number of bacteria and t is the number of hours.

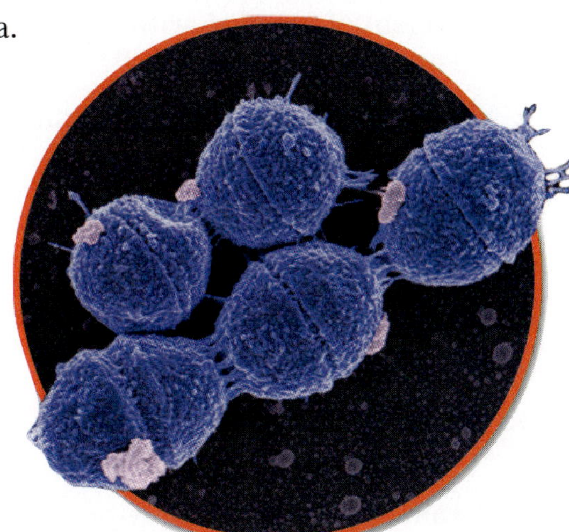

a. What is the population of the colony after 3 hours? After 5 hours?

b. What mathematical operations did you perform to calculate your answers in part (a)? In what order did you perform these operations?

Write an expression equivalent to the given expression.

26. $5 - 6(x + 10) - 4$

27. $-3(x - 4) - (x + 3)$

28. $x(x + 2) - 5x + 6$

29. $6x^2 + 5x(x - 10) + 10$

30. $\frac{1}{2}x^2 + \frac{1}{4}x^2 + x^2 + 3x$

31. $7x^2 - 3.5x + 0.75x - 8$

For: Multiple-Choice Skills Practice
Web Code: apa-6454

32. Write an equation for

a. y in terms of z given $y = 6x +$

b. P in terms of n given $P = xn -$

c. A in terms of w given $A = \ell w$ a

For Exercises 33–35, give an equation f

33. a parabola with x-intercepts $(-3, 0$

34. a line with a slope of -4 and an x-i

35. an exponential function with a gro

36. a. Sketch each equation on the sa

$y = 4x^2$ $\qquad y = -4x^2$

b. What is the effect of the variabl

37. a. Sketch each equation on the sa

$y = 4x^2 + 5$ $\qquad y = 4x^2 - 5$

b. What is the effect of the variabl

38. You want to tie the anchor wire of distance that is half the height of th tallest flagpole you can support wit

39. The figures show cones inside cylin height. Which cone has a volume of

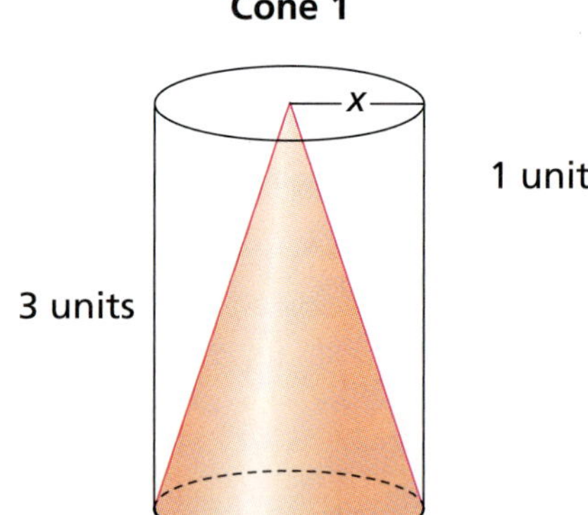

42. a. Graph $y = x^2 + 4$. Is it possible to find x when $y = 0$? Explain.

b. Give two examples of a quadratic equation ($ax^2 + bx + c = 0$, where a, b, and c are real numbers) with no solution.

c. Give two examples of a quadratic equation with 1 solution.

d. Give two examples of a quadratic equation with 2 solutions.

43. Below is the graph of $y = (x + 2)(x - 1)(x - 5)$. The scale on the x-axis is 1. The scale on the y-axis is 5.

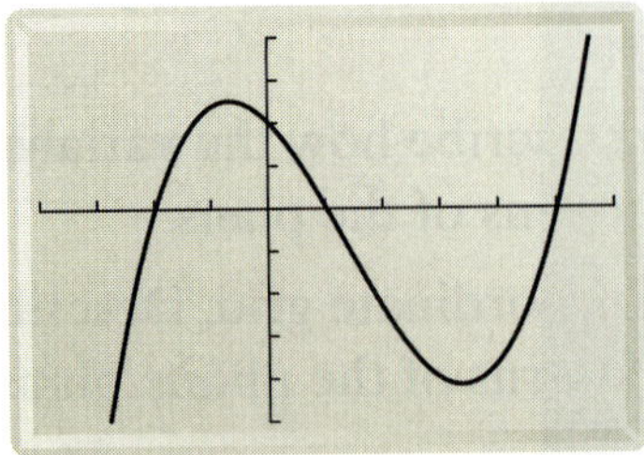

a. What are the solutions to $(x + 2)(x - 1)(x - 5) = 0$? How are the solutions shown on the graph?

b. What values of x satisfy the inequality $(x + 2)(x - 1)(x - 5) < 0$? How is your answer shown on the graph?

c. How can you find the answer to part (b) without using the graph?

Mathematical Reflections 4

In this investigation, you studied equations that represent linear, exponential, or quadratic functions. You also used expanded or factored expressions for *y* to make predictions about the shape of the graph of these functions. These questions will help you summarize what you have learned.

Think about your answers to these questions. Discuss your ideas with other students and your teacher. Then write a summary of your findings in your notebook.

1. Describe how you can tell whether an equation is a linear, exponential, or quadratic function. Include the factored or expanded form of the expression for y.
2. Describe how you can determine specific features of the graph of a function from its equation. Include its shape, x- and y-intercepts, maximum and minimum points, and patterns of change.

Investigation 5

Reasoning With Symbols

You have looked at patterns and made conjectures and predictions. You have given informal arguments to support your conjectures. In this investigation, you will look at how algebra can help you further justify some of your conjectures by providing evidence or proof.

5.1 Using Algebra to Solve a Puzzle

People receive a lot of information by email. Some emails are useful, while others are for fun. A puzzle similar to the following appeared in several emails in 2003.

Problem 5.1 Using Algebra to Solve a Puzzle

On February 1, 2006, Elizabeth shared the following puzzle with her classmates.

- Pick a number from 1 to 9.
- Multiply this number by 2.
- Add 5.
- Multiply by 50.
- If you already had your birthday this year, add 1,756. If not, add 1,755.
- Subtract the four-digit year in which you were born.

A. 1. Suppose the year is 2006. Work through the steps using today's month and day.

2. You should have a three-digit number. Look at the first digit and the last two digits. What information do these numbers represent?

B. Let n represent the number you choose in the first step. Repeat the steps with n. Use mathematical statements to explain why the puzzle works.

C. Will the puzzle work for the current year? If not, how can you change the steps to make it work?

ACE **Homework starts on page 76.**

5.2 Odd and Even Revisited

In *Prime Time,* you looked at factors and multiples. You explored several conjectures about even and odd whole numbers, including:

- The sum of two even whole numbers is even.
- The sum of an even whole number and odd whole number is odd.

How might you convince a friend that these conjectures are true?

Are these conjectures true for odd and even integers?

Getting Ready for Problem 

Daphne claims that the algebraic expression $2n$, where n is any integer, will produce all even integers.

- Is Daphne correct? Explain.
- Write a symbolic expression that will produce all odd integers. Explain why it works.

Problem 5.2 Odd and Even Revisited

Rachel offers the following argument for showing that the sum of two even integers is even.

- Let n and m represent any integer.
- Then $2n$ and $2m$ are two even integers.
- $2n + 2m$ is the sum of two even integers.
- But $2n + 2m = 2(n + m)$.
- $2(n + m)$ is an even integer.
- So the sum of two even integers is even.

A. Study Rachel's argument. Provide reasons for each step. Does her argument prove the conjecture that the sum of any two even integers is an even integer? Explain.

B. Bianca offers the following argument:

- You can represent even numbers as a rectangular array with one dimension equal to 2. The following pictures represent the sum of two even numbers.

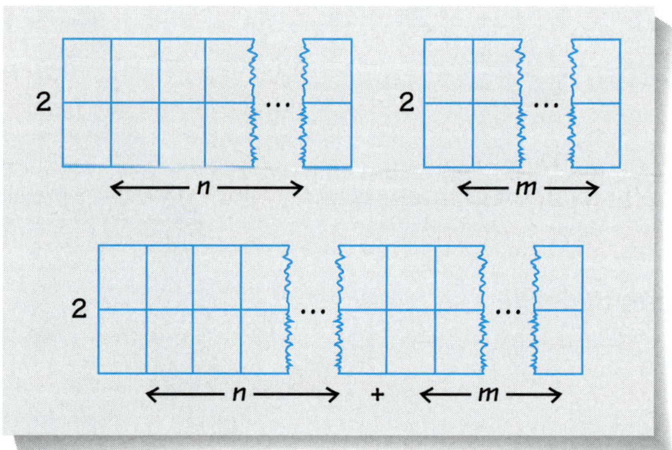

Does Bianca's argument prove the conjecture about the sum of two even numbers? Explain.

C. Use a method similar to those in Questions A and B to show that the following conjectures are true.

1. The sum of an odd integer and an even integer is an odd integer.

2. The product of an even and an odd integer is even.

ACE Homework starts on page 76.

5.3 Squaring Odd Numbers

In this problem, you will operate on odd numbers and look for patterns.

Problem 5.3 Squaring Odd Numbers

A. Perform the following operations on the first eight odd numbers. Record your information in a table.

- Pick an odd number.
- Square it.
- Subtract 1.

B. What patterns do you see in the resulting numbers?

C. Make conjectures about these numbers. Explain why your conjectures are true for any odd number.

ACE Homework starts on page 76.

Applications

Connections

Extensions

Applications

Maria presents several number puzzles to her friends. She asks them to think of a number and to perform various operations on it. She then predicts the result. For Exercises 1 and 2, show why the puzzles work.

1.

Puzzle 1

- Pick a number.
- Double it.
- Add 6.
- Divide by 2.
- Subtract the number you thought of.

Maria claims the result is 3.

2.

Puzzle 2

- Think of a number.
- Add 4.
- Multiply by 2.
- Subtract 6.
- Divide by 2.
- Subtract the number you thought of.

Maria claims the result is 1.

3. **a.** Design a puzzle similar to Maria's puzzles.

b. Try it on a friend.

c. Explain why your puzzle works.

For Exercises 4–6, show that the following conjectures are true.

4. The sum of two odd integers is even.

5. The product of two even integers is even.

6. The product of two odd integers is odd.

7. Look at the product of three consecutive whole numbers. For example:

$1 \times 2 \times 3 \qquad 2 \times 3 \times 4 \qquad 3 \times 4 \times 5$

   a. What patterns do you observe?

   b. Make a conjecture about the product of three consecutive whole numbers. Explain why your conjecture is correct.

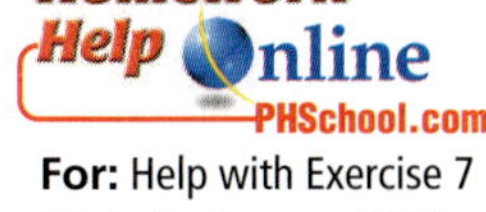

For: Help with Exercise 7
Web Code: ape-6507

8. Look at the product of four consecutive whole numbers.

   a. What patterns do you observe?

   b. Make a conjecture about the product of four consecutive whole numbers. Explain why your conjecture is correct.

9. a. Are the following numbers divisible by 2? Explain.

10,034 69,883

   b. What patterns among these numbers do you notice that can help you determine whether a number is divisible by 2?

   c. Explain your conclusion.

10. a. Look at several numbers that are divisible by 4.

   b. What patterns among these numbers do you notice that can help you determine whether a number is divisible by 4?

   c. Explain your conclusion.

11. a. Look at several numbers that are divisible by 5.

   b. What patterns among these numbers do you notice that can help you determine whether a number is divisible by 5?

   c. Explain your conclusion.

Connections

12. Study the sequence of cube buildings below.

- What pattern do you notice?
- Use the pattern to construct the next building in the sequence.
- Think about your steps as you construct your building. The labels below show one way you might think about the pattern.

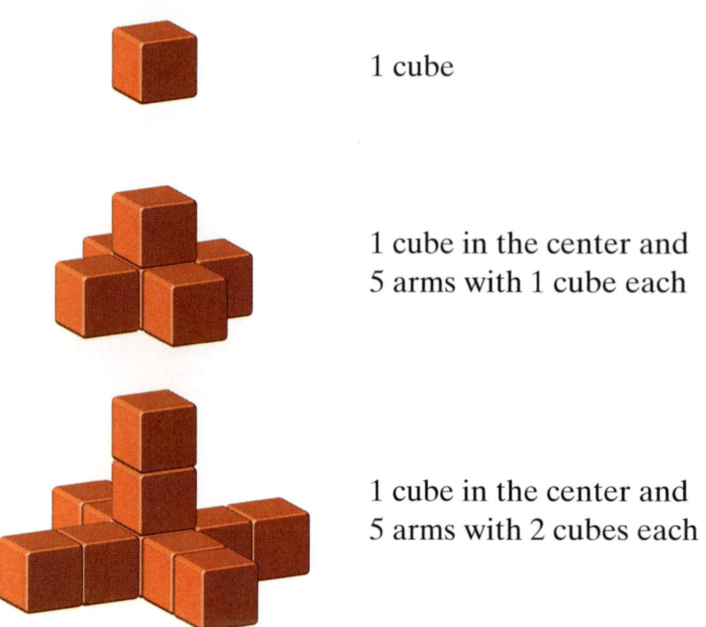

a. Describe a pattern you see in the cube buildings.

b. Use your pattern to write an expression for the number of cubes in the nth building, where n is an integer.

c. Use your expression to find the number of cubes in the fifth building.

d. Use the Distributive and Commutative properties to write an expression equivalent to the one in part (b). Does this expression suggest another pattern in the cube buildings? Explain.

e. Look for a different pattern in the buildings. Describe the pattern and use it to write a different expression for the number of cubes in the nth building.

For Exercises 13 and 14, suppose a chess tournament has *n* participants. Each participant plays each of the other participants twice.

13. a. Find the total number of games played for tournaments with 2, 3, 4, 5, and 6 participants.

b. Look for a pattern in your data. Use the pattern to write an expression for the number of games played in a tournament with *n* participants.

14. Gina used a table to answer Exercise 13. Make a table like the one below to record wins (W) and losses (L) for a tournament with *n* participants.

Game 1 (columns); **Game 2** (rows)

	P_1	P_2	P_3	...	P_n
P_1					
P_2					
P_3					
...					
P_n					

a. How many cells should your table have?

b. How many cells in the table will not be used? Explain.

c. Use your answers from parts (a) and (b) to write an expression for the total number of games played.

d. Compare your expressions for the total number of games played in Exercises 13(b) and 14(c).

Connections

For Exercises 15–18, answer parts (a) and (b) below.

a. Write an equation to represent each situation.

b. Write a problem that can be solved by substituting a value into the equation. Then solve your problem.

15. Suppose you go on an 8-hour car trip. You travel at an average rate of r miles per hour for the first 6 hours on the highway and at an average rate of 30 mph slower for the last 2 hours in the city. Find the distance traveled.

16. Suppose a bag contains only dimes and quarters. The bag has 1,000 coins. Find the amount of money in the bag.

17. Suppose the length of a rectangular pool is 4 feet longer than twice the width. Find the area of the pool.

18. Suppose that for a concert, there are x reserved seats that cost \$15 per seat and $(4{,}000 - x)$ unreserved seats that cost \$9 per seat. The concert sells out. Find the amount of money collected for the concert.

Solve each equation for *x* without using a table or a graph.

19. $(x - 4)(x + 3) = 0$

20. $x^2 + 4x = 0$

21. $x^2 + 9x + 20 = 0$

22. $x^2 + 7x - 8 = 0$

23. $x^2 - 11x + 10 = 0$

24. $x^2 - 6x - 27 = 0$

25. $x^2 - 25 = 0$

26. $x^2 - 100 = 0$

27. $2x^2 + 3x + 1 = 0$

28. $3x^2 + 10x + 8 = 0$

Go Online
PHSchool.com
For: Multiple-Choice Skills Practice
Web Code: apa-6554

29. The height of a ball (in feet) t seconds after it is thrown is $h = -16t^2 + 48t$. Find each without using a table or graph.

a. the height of the ball after 2 seconds

b. the maximum height of the ball

c. the total time the ball is in the air

d. How could you use a table or graph to answer parts (a)–(c)? Explain.

For Exercises 30 and 31, write an equation of the form y = *expression* for each expression. Show whether the two expressions are or are not equivalent

(a) with a table and graph.

(b) without a table or graph.

30. $9x - 5(x - 3) - 20$ and $5 - 4x$

31. $(10x - 5) - (4x + 2)$ and $10x - 5 - 4x + 2$

For Exercises 32–36, complete each table without using a calculator. Decide whether the relationship is linear, quadratic, exponential, or none of these.

32.

x	5	−5	−3	−7
$y = 4(x - 7) + 6$	■	■	■	■

33.

x	5	−5	−3	−7
$y = -3 - 7(x + 9)$	■	■	■	■

34.

x	5	−5	−3	−7
$y = 2(3)^x$	■	■	■	■

35.

x	5	−5	−3	−7
$y = 3x^2 - x - 1$	■	■	■	■

36.

x	5	−5	−3	−7
$y = 5(x - 2)(x + 3)$	■	■	■	■

37. For Exercises 32 and 33, write an equivalent expression for y that would make the calculations easier.

Connections

38. Study the pattern in each table. Write an equation for those that are linear, exponential, or quadratic. Otherwise, write *none of these*.

Table 1

x	y
−2	15
0	9
2	3
3	0
4	−3

Table 2

x	y
0	−16
1	−15
2	−12
3	−7
4	0

Table 3

x	y
−2	2
−1	1
0	0
1	1
2	2

Table 4

x	y
0	3
1	12
2	48
3	192
4	768

Table 5

x	y
1	4
2	2
3	$\frac{4}{3}$
4	1
5	$\frac{4}{5}$

Extensions

39. a. Find the next statement for the following pattern.

$$1^2 + 2^2 = 3^2 - 2^2$$
$$2^2 + 3^2 = 7^2 - 6^2$$
$$3^2 + 4^2 = 13^2 - 12^2$$
$$4^2 + 5^2 = 21^2 - 20^2$$

b. Make a conjecture about these statements.

c. Show that your conjecture is correct.

40. For many years, mathematicians have been looking for a way to generate prime numbers. One of their proposed rules follows.

$$P = n^2 - n + 41$$

The rule suggests that if n is a whole number, then $n^2 - n + 41$ is a prime number.

George claims the rule is not true because he tested it for several values of n and found one that did not yield a prime number.

a. Test the rule for several values of n. Is each result prime?

b. Is George correct? Explain.

41. a. Look at several numbers that are divisible by 3.

b. What patterns among these numbers do you notice that can help you determine whether a number is divisible by 3?

c. Explain why your method works.

42. a. Look at several numbers that are divisible by 6.

b. What patterns among these numbers do you notice that can help you determine whether a number is divisible by 6?

c. Explain why your method works.

43. Judy thinks she knows a quick way to square any number whose last digit is 5. (Example: 25)

- Look at the digit to the left of 5. Multiply it by the number that is one greater than this number. (Example: $2 \times 3 = 6$)
- Write the product followed by 25. This is the square of the number. (Example: 625 is the square of 25.)

a. Try this squaring method on two other numbers that end in 5.

b. Explain why this method works.

Mathematical Reflections 5

In this investigation, you made conjectures about patterns that you observed and represented these conjectures in symbolic statements. You also found ways to show that your conjectures were valid.

Think about your answers to this question. Discuss your ideas with other students and your teacher. Then write a summary of your findings in your notebook.

1. Describe how and why you could use symbolic statements to show relationships or generalizations.
2. Describe how you can show that your generalizations are correct.

Unit Project

Finding the Surface Area of Rod Stacks

In this unit project, you will find different ways to find the surface area of colored rod stacks.

Part 1: Staircase Stacks

1. Choose a rod length to use to make a staircase stack. Use one of the unit rods to determine the dimensions of your chosen rod.
2. Stack several rods of this length as shown. Each rod is one unit high and one unit wide and is staggered one unit.

Stacked Rods **Unit Rod**

Find the surface area of one rod, a stack of two rods, a stack of three rods, and so on. Describe a pattern that you see in the surface areas of the stacks you made.

3. Write an equation that shows the relationship between the surface area A and the number of rods n in the stack. Explain.
4. Repeat Exercises 1–3 for two other rod lengths.
5. Find a student who used rods of the same length for Exercises 1–3 and whose expression from Exercise 3 looks different from yours. Are your expressions equivalent? Explain.

6. **a.** Make a table with columns for rod length and surface area equation. Complete the table for rod lengths 2 through 10. You will need to find students who used rods that you didn't use.

   b. Do the equations in your table represent linear, quadratic, or exponential relationships? Explain.

   c. Write an equation for the surface area A of any stack of n rods of length ℓ.

   d. Use your equation from part (c) to find the surface area of a stack of 50 rods of length 10.

Part 2: Finding the Surface Area of a Rectangular Prism

Suppose rods of length 4 are stacked to form a rectangular prism as shown at the right.

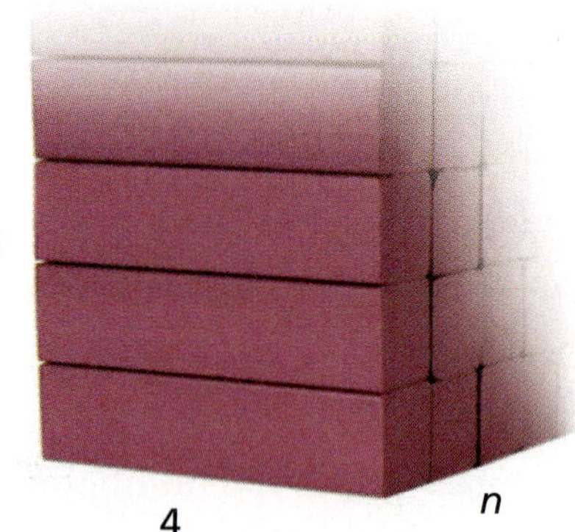

7. What are the dimensions of the prism?

8. Find an equation for the surface area of the prism.

9. Suppose the prism is 10 rods high and 10 rods wide. What is the surface area of the prism?

10. How would the equation change if the rod length were something other than 4?

11. Is the relationship between the surface area and the number of rods in a prism stack linear, quadratic, exponential, or none of these? Explain.

Write a report about the results you found for rod stacks and rod prisms. Explain how you found the equations for surface area in each case. Use diagrams to show what you did and what you found.

Looking Back and Looking Ahead

Unit Review

In this unit, you learned and practiced the standard rules for using symbolic expressions in algebra. You used properties of numbers and operations to write algebraic expressions in equivalent forms and to solve linear and quadratic equations with algebraic reasoning.

For: Vocabulary Review Puzzle
Web Code: apj-6051

Use Your Understanding: Symbols

Test your understanding and skill in the use of algebraic notation and reasoning by solving these problems about managing a concert tour.

The promoter pays appearance fees to each group on the concert program. Some groups also get a portion of the ticket sales.

- The lead group earns $15,000, plus $5 for every ticket sold.
- Another group earns $1,500, plus $1.50 for every ticket sold.
- The third group earns a flat fee of $1,250.

1. For parts (a)–(c), use E for the promoter's expenses and t for the number of tickets sold.

a. Write an equation to show payments to each separate group.

b. Write an equation to show payment to the lead group and the combined payments to the other groups.

c. Write an equivalent equation different from parts (a) and (b) to show the simplest calculation of the total amount paid to the performers.

2. Tickets cost $25, $30, and $40.

a. Write an equation that shows how the promoter's income from ticket sales I depends on the number of each type of ticket sold x, y, and z.

b. The promoter sells 5,000 tickets at $25, 3,000 tickets at $30, and 950 tickets at $40. Find the average income per ticket.

c. Write an equation that shows how the average income per ticket sold V depends on the variables x, y, z, and t.

3. Square tiles were used to make the pattern below.

a. Write an equation for the number of tiles T needed to make the nth figure. Explain.

b. Find an equivalent expression for the number of tiles in part (a). Explain why they are equivalent.

c. Write an equation for the perimeter P of the nth figure.

d. Identify and describe the figure in this pattern that can be made with exactly 420 tiles.

e. Describe the relationship represented by the equations in parts (a) and (c).

Explain Your Reasoning

When you solve problems by writing and operating on symbolic expressions, you should be able to explain your reasoning.

4. How can writing two different equivalent expressions or equations for a situation be helpful?

5. How can solving a linear or quadratic equation be helpful?

6. How can a symbolic statement be helpful in expressing a general relationship or conjecture?

Look Ahead

The algebraic ideas and techniques you have used in this unit will be applied and extended in future mathematics courses and in science and business problems.

In later mathematics courses you will explore more techniques for solving quadratic and polynomial equations. You will also learn how to write equivalent expressions using more properties of real numbers.

English / Spanish Glossary

C

Commutative Property of Addition A mathematical property that states that the order in which quantities are added does not matter. It states that $a + b = b + a$ for any two real numbers a and b. For example, $5 + 7 = 7 + 5$ and $2x + 4 = 4 + 2x$.

propiedad conmutativa de la suma Una propiedad matemática que dice que el orden en que se suman las cantidades no tiene importancia. Para cualquieres números reales a y b, $a + b = b + a$. Por ejemplo, $5 + 7 = 7 + 5$ y $2x + 4 = 4 + 2x$.

Commutative Property of Multiplication A mathematical property that states that the order in which quantities are multiplied does not matter. It states that $ab = ba$ for any two real numbers a and b. For example, $5 \times 7 = 7 \times 5$ and $2x(4) = (4)2x$.

propiedad conmutativa de la multiplicación Una propiedad matemática que dice que el orden en que se multiplican los factores no tiene importancia. Para cualquieres números reales, $ab = ba$. Por ejemplo, $5 \times 7 = 7 \times 5$ y $2x(4) = (4)2x$.

D

Distributive Property A mathematical property used to rewrite expressions involving addition and multiplication. The Distributive Property states that for any three real numbers a, b, and c, $a(b + c) = ab + ac$. If an expression is written as a factor multiplied by a sum, you can use the Distributive Property to *multiply* the factor by each term in the sum.

$$4(5 + x) = 4(5) + 4(x) = 20 + 4x$$

If an expression is written as a sum of terms and the terms have a common factor, you can use the Distributive Property to rewrite the expression as the common factor multiplied by a sum. This process is called *factoring*.

$$20 + 4x = 4(5) + 4(x) = 4(5 + x)$$

propiedad distributiva Una propiedad matemática usada para reescribir expresiones que incluyen la suma y la multiplicación. La propiedad distributiva se establece para cualquieres números reales a, b, y c, $a(b + c) = ab + ac$. Si una expresión se escribe como la multiplicación de un factor por una suma, la propiedad distributiva puede usarse para multiplicar el factor por cada término de la suma.

$$4(5 + x) = 4(5) + 4(x) = 20 + 4x$$

Si una expresión se escribe como la suma de los términos y los términos tienen un factor común, la propiedad distributiva puede usarse para reescribir o descomponer en factores la expresión como la multiplicación del factor común por una suma.

$$20 + 4x = 4(5) + 4(x) = 4(5 + x)$$

E

equivalent expressions Expressions that represent the same quantity. For example, $2 + 5$, $3 + 4$, and 7 are equivalent expressions. You can apply the Distributive Property to $2(x + 3)$ to write the equivalent expression $2x + 6$. You can apply the Commutative Property to $2x + 6$ to write the equivalent expression $6 + 2x$.

expresiones equivalentes Expresiones que representan la misma cantidad, como por ejemplo $2 + 5$, $3 + 4$ y 7. Puedes aplicar la propiedad distributive a $2(x + 3)$ para escribir la expresión equivalente $2x + 6$. Puedes aplicar la propiedad conmutativa a $2x + 6$ para escribir la expresión equivalente $6 + 2x$.

expanded form The form of an expression made up of sums or differences of terms rather than products of factors. The expressions $x^2 + 7x + 12$ and $x^2 + 2x$ are in expanded form.

forma desarrollada La forma de una expresión compuesta de sumas o diferencias de términos en vez de productos de factores. Las expresiones $x^2 + 7x + 12$ y $x^2 + 2x$ están representadas en forma desarrollada.

F

factored form The form of an expression made up of products of factors rather than sums or differences of terms. The expressions $(x + 3)(x + 4)$ and $x(x - 2)$ are in factored form.

forma de factores La forma de una expresión compuesta de productos de factores en vez de sumas o diferencias de términos. Las expresiones $(x + 3)(x + 4)$ y $x(x - 2)$ están representadas en forma de factores.

P

parabola The graph of a quadratic function. A parabola has a line of symmetry that passes through the maximum point if the graph opens downward or through the minimum point if the graph opens upward.

parábola La gráfica de una función cuadrática. Una parábola tiene un eje de simetría que pasa por el punto máximo si la gráfica se abre hacia abajo o por el punto mínimo si la gráfica se abre hacia arriba.

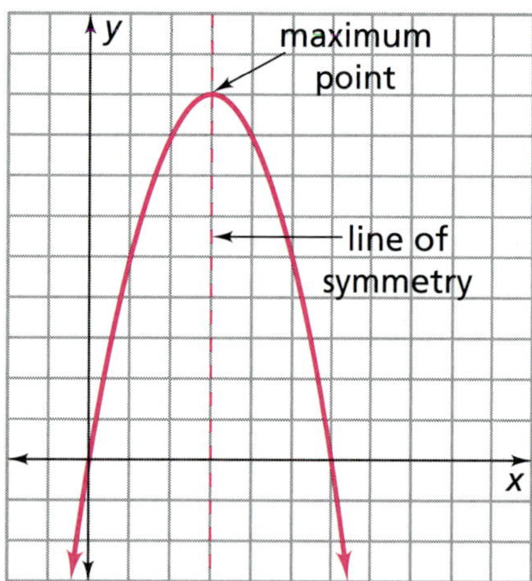

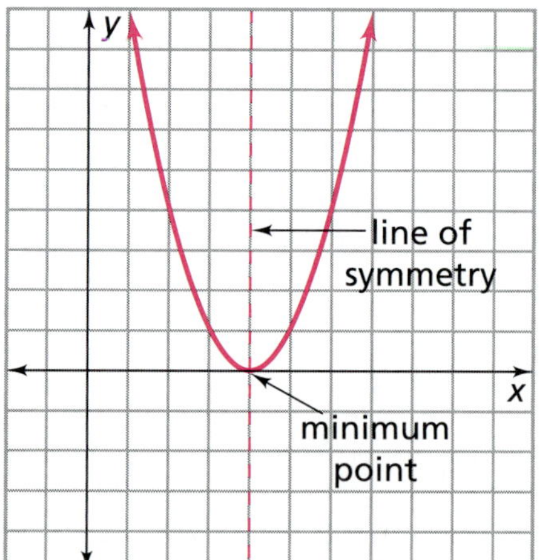

properties of equality The properties of equality state that if you add or subtract both sides of an equation by the same number, the two sides of the equation remain equal. If you multiply or divide both sides of an equation by the same non-zero number, the two sides of the equation remain equal.

propiedades de igualdad Las propiedades de igualdad establecen que si se suma o resta el mismo número a ambos lados de una ecuación, los dos lados de la ecuación se mantienen iguales. Si ambos lados de una ecuación se multiplican o dividen por el mismo número distinto de cero, los dos lados de la ecuación se mantienen iguales.

R

roots The roots of an equation are the values of x that make y equal 0. For example, the roots of $y = x^2 + 5x$ are -5 and 0 because $(-5)^2 + 5(-5) = 0$ and $0^2 + 5(0) = 0$. The roots of $y = x^2 + 5x$ are the solutions to the equation $0 = x^2 + 5x$. The roots of an equation are the x-intercepts of its graph.

raíces Las raíces de una ecuación son los valores de x que hacen que y equivalga a 0. Por ejemplo, las raíces de $y = x^2 + 5x$ son -5 y 0 porque $(-5)^2 + 5(-5) = 0$ y $0^2 + 5(0) = 0$. Las raíces de $y = x^2 + 5x$ son las soluciones de la ecuación $0 = x^2 + 5x$. Las raíces de una ecuación son los puntos de intersección del eje de las x de la gráfica de esa ecuación.

T

term An expression with numbers and/or variables multiplied together. In the expression $3x^2 - 2x + 10$, $3x^2$, $-2x$, and 10 are terms.

término Una expresión con números y/o variables multiplicados entre sí. En la expresión $3x^2 - 2x + 10$, $3x^2$, $-2x$, y 10 son términos.

Academic Vocabulary

The following terms are important to your understanding of the mathematics in this unit. Knowing and using these words will help you in thinking, reasoning, representing, communicating your ideas, and making connections across ideas. When these words make sense to you, the investigations and problems will make more sense as well.

D

describe To explain or tell in detail. A written description can contain facts and other information needed to communicate your answer. A diagram or a graph may also be included.

related terms: *express, explain, illustrate*

Sample: Without graphing, describe the shape of the graph of the equation $y = 2x^2 + 1$.

The equation is quadratic so the graph is a parabola. The graph opens upward because 2 is positive. It is narrower than the graph of $y = x^2$ because the absolute value of 2 is greater than 1.

describir Explicar o decir con detalle. Una descripción escrita puede contener hechos y otra información necesaria para comunicar tu respuesta. También se puede incluir un diagrama o una gráfica.

términos relacionados: *expresar, explicar, ilustrar*

Ejemplo: Sin hacer la gráfica, describe la forma de la gráfica de la ecuación $y = 2x^2 + 1$.

La ecuación es cuadrática así que la gráfica es una parábola. La gráfica se abre hacia arriba porque 2 es positivo. Es más estrecha que la gráfica de $y = x^2$ porque el valor absoluto de 2 es mayor que 1.

E

estimate To find an approximate answer.

related terms: *guess, predict*

Sample: Estimate the lateral surface area of the net of the cone below.

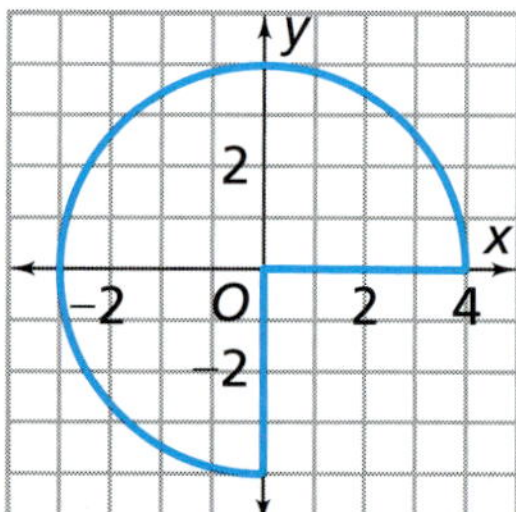

I can count the number of unit squares. The net of the cone has 3 equal sections. I estimate one of the sections to be 13 square units, so the total is about 39 square units.

estimar Hallar una respuesta aproximada.

términos relacionados: *conjeturar, predecir*

Ejemplo: Estima el área lateral de la plantilla del cono que sigue.

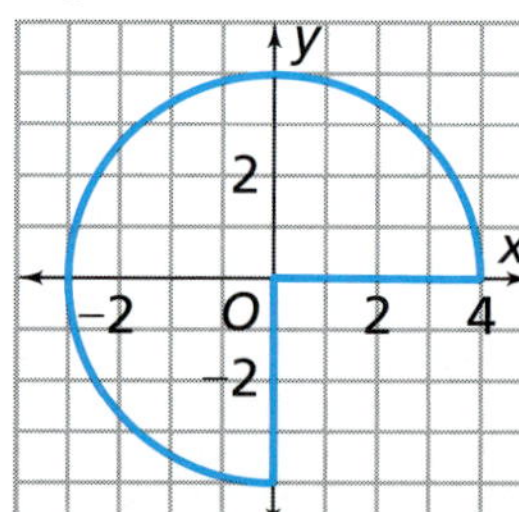

Puedo contar el número de unidades cuadradas. La plantilla del cono tiene 3 secciones iguales. Estimo que una de las secciones tiene aproximadamente 13 unidades cuadradas, por tanto el total es aproximadamente 39 unidades cuadradas.

explain To give facts and details that make an idea easier to understand. Explaining can involve a written summary supported by a diagram, chart, table, or a combination of these.
related terms: *analyze, clarify, describe, justify, tell*

Sample: The equation shows the relationship between the number of gallons g of water in a tank and the number of minutes m a shower is on.

$$g = 50 - 2.5m$$

How many gallons of water are in a full tank before the shower begins? Explain.

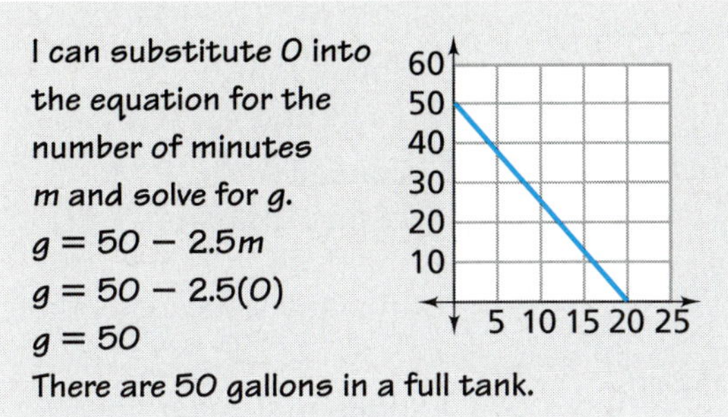

explicar Dar hechos y detalles que hacen que una idea sea más fácil de comprender. Explicar puede implicar un resumen escrito apoyado por un diagrama, una gráfica, una tabla o una combinación de éstos.
términos relacionados: *analizar, aclarar, describir, justificar, decir*

Ejemplo: La ecuación muestra la relación entre el número de galones g de agua en un tanque y el número de minutos m que ha estado funcionando una ducha.

$$g = 50 - 2.5m$$

¿Cuántos galones de agua hay en un tanque lleno antes que comience la ducha? Explica tu respuesta.

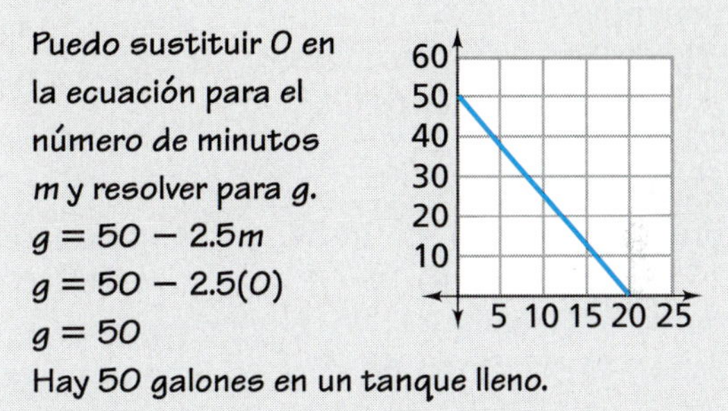

S

solve To determine the value or values that make a given statement true. Several methods and strategies can be used to solve a problem including estimating, isolating the variable, drawing a graph, or using a table of values.
related terms: *find, graph*

Sample: Solve the equation for x.
$0 = x^2 + 6x - 7$.

The equation is quadratic. I can solve the equation by factoring the right side of the equation into two factors and setting each factor equal to zero.

$0 = x^2 + 6x - 7$

$0 = (x + 7)(x - 1)$

$x + 7 = 0$ or $x - 1 = 0$

$x = -7$ or $x = 1$

I can also solve the quadratic by graphing and identifying the x-intercepts at $(-7, 0)$ and $(1, 0)$.

(-7, 0) (1, 0)

resolver Determinar el valor o valores que hacen cierto un enunciado dado. Pueden usarse varios métodos y estrategias para resolver un problema incluyendo estimar, despejar la variable, dibujar una gráfica o usar una tabla de valores.
términos relacionados *hallar, hacer una gráfica*

Ejemplo: Resuelve la ecuación para x.
$0 = x^2 + 6x - 7$.

La ecuación es cuadrática. Puedo resolver la ecuación factorizando el lado derecho de la ecuación en dos factores y estableciendo cada factor igual a cero.

$0 = x^2 + 6x - 7$

$0 = (x + 7)(x - 1)$

$x + 7 = 0$ or $x - 1 = 0$

$x = -7$ or $x = 1$

También puedo resolver la ecuación cuadrática al hacer una gráfica e identificar los interceptos de x en $(-7, 0)$ y $(1, 0)$.

(-7, 0) (1, 0)

Index

Index

Acknowledgments

Team Credits

The people who made up the **Connected Mathematics 2** team —representing editorial, editorial services, design services, and production services— are listed below. Bold type denotes core team members.

Leora Adler, Judith Buice, Kerry Cashman, Patrick Culleton, Sheila DeFazio, Richard Heater, **Barbara Hollingdale, Jayne Holman,** Karen Holtzman, **Etta Jacobs,** Christine Lee, Carolyn Lock, Catherine Maglio, **Dotti Marshall,** Rich McMahon, Eve Melnechuk, Kristin Mingrone, Terri Mitchell, **Marsha Novak,** Irene Rubin, Donna Russo, Robin Samper, Siri Schwartzman, **Nancy Smith,** Emily Soltanoff, **Mark Tricca,** Paula Vergith, Roberta Warshaw, Helen Young

Additional Credits

Diana Bonfilio, Mairead Reddin, Michael Torocsik, nSight, Inc.

Technical Illustration

WestWords, Inc.

Cover Design

tom white.images

Photos

2, Tom Carter/PhotoEdit; **3,** Elio Ciol/Corbis; **5,** Ryan McVay/PictureQuest; **10,** Photodisc/Getty Images, Inc.; **14,** Tim Kiusalaas/Masterfile; **17,** Jeff Greenberg/AGE Fotostock; **19,** Jules Frazier/PictureQuest; **21,** Richard Haynes; **23,** Michael Mancuso/Omni-Photo Communications, Inc.; **26,** Jeff Greenberg/Omni-Photo Communications, Inc.; **27,** Photodisc/Getty Images, Inc.; **29,** Stephen Simpson/Getty Images, Inc.; **30,** Terry W. Eggers/Corbis; **33,** Syracuse Newspapers/The Image Works; **35,** Jeff Greenberg/The Image Works; **41,** Richard Haynes; **43,** Dennis MacDonald/PhotoEdit; **44,** Francois Viete (1540–1603) (engraving) (b/w photo), French School, (19th century)/Private Collection, Lauros/Giraudon/www.bridgeman.co.uk; **47,** Tom Carter/PhotoEdit; **52,** Syracuse Newspapers/Al Campanie/The Image Works; **58,** David Young-Wolff/PhotoEdit; **61,** Lester Lefkowitz/Getty Images, Inc.; **62,** Tom Brakefield/Corbis; **67,** Dr. Gary Gaugler/Photo Researchers, Inc.; **69,** Spencer Platt/Getty Images, Inc.; **73,** Richard Haynes; **79,** Esbin/Anderson/Omni-Photo Communications, Inc.; **83,** Richard Haynes; **85,** Russ Lappa; **86,** Russ Lappa